Watermelon is Life

Invaluable Lessons From
Teaching English Abroad

WES WESTON

Watermelon is Life
Invaluable Lessons from Teaching English Abroad

Copyright © 2013 by Wes Weston

Cover Design by Clarissa Yeo

For further information please contact the author at DoUEnglish@gmail.com.

I have tried to recreate events, locales, and conversations from my memories of them. In order to maintain anonymity, in some instances I have changed the names of individuals and places.

PROVIDING THE KEY TO
PRIMARY EDUCATION IN AFRICA

Unlock Foundation is a non-profit organization that seeks to address critical educational gaps in rural African schools. They work with teachers, students and community members on small sustainable projects that ensure students receive the best primary education possible.

For every copy of *Watermelon is Life* that is purchased, one dollar will be donated to the Unlock Foundation. You can find out more information about the Unlock Foundation at **www.UnlockFoundation.org**. Thank you for your support!

This book is dedicated to the school learners of Namibia. To all those kids who are enduring countless obstacles to secure themselves an education, keep pushing yourselves to succeed. You inspire me to no end.

CONTENTS

Chapter 22 – Enda Po Nawa!

It's hard to say goodbye, but this day was coming.

Chapter 23 – Be the Change You Wish to See in the World

The author discovers that perhaps one person can't change the world, but the world can certainly change one person.

Epilogue - Synchronicity

The pathway of life takes a turn in a new direction. This time, it's leading the author to some place tropical.

Acknowledgements

Just giving some much deserved praise to those who contributed to this book.

About the Author

Oh so vain!

References

The author cites all the sources he has plagiarized.

Endnotes

Additional information for the reader.

Do U English?

I am an English teacher, and I have a bone to pick with English. I'm probably not the only one. I try to teach ***proper English***, yet I'm beginning to question whether this very notion is an oxymoron. "Proper English." Do these words go together? Or, are they slowly becoming polar opposites, along with phrases like "living dead", "serious joke", and "irregular pattern"? The word *proper*, when used as an adjective to modify a noun, means *genuine or truly what something is said to be*. Can a language be an absolute?

The English language is constantly changing. So how do you determine what counts as English? Should slang be included? Some people hella think so! What about different vernaculars of English? Americans use different words than Brits. Our varieties of English are so colourful that we even spell words differently. How about words that we have taken from other languages? The word *fiancé* is a French word that has been accepted into English. Spanish words like *fiesta* and *siesta* have recently been adopted into American English. You can find them entered in just about any modern English dictionary. Are these words I should be teaching?

The *Oxford English Dictionary* is one of the premiere English dictionaries. Perhaps its greatest criticism is the alleged authority it exerts over the usage of English. The dictionary's history began in 1879 with James Murray, a British scholar who began work on a *New English Dictionary*. Sadly, Murray passed away in 1915 and did not see the completion of his work. But after 53 years of toil, *A New English*

Dictionary on Historic Principles was completed in 1928 and represented a publishing achievement that was unprecedented. It contained over 400,000 entries within 10 volumes. Years later, in 1933, a supplement was published, which formally became the First Edition of the *Oxford English Dictionary*.

At the time, the problem was quite clear. How do you maintain a living language? Essentially, your work never ends. Thus, editors, scholars, and lexicographers continued to update and revise the English language. The Second Edition of the *Oxford English Dictionary* was published in 1989 as 20 volumes, and it contained over 600,000 entries. But wait, it gets better. So as not to become outdated, work on the Third Edition of the *Oxford English Dictionary* began in the mid-1990s. Originally scheduled for release in 2010, that date has since been pushed back to somewhere around 2037. This latest edition is expected to include 40 volumes and have over 900,000 entries. If that's the case, one could argue that English has more than doubled in size in the last 100 years. ***Booyah!*** It's okay; I can use this word as an expression of joy because it is listed in the dictionary as an interjection.

English – for lack of a better way of putting it – is a monster. Many believe it contains more words than any other language on the planet, although this argument is unlikely to ever be proven. Yet how can such a complex and ever-emerging language such as English lack basic coherence? For example, one of the biggest gripes I have with English is gender neutrality. When I write, I use the pronoun *they* as singular, and I do it frequently throughout this book. Let me give you an example. If <u>*someone*</u> is reading this, perhaps <u>*they*</u> could not care less about gender-neutral pronouns. *Someone* is a singular noun that I conveniently replaced with the plural pronoun *they*. Now a professor from the School of Journalism may say that *he or she* is the correct usage. Or it's acceptable for the author to use his or her own gender to represent a gender neutral pronoun. Since I am a man, then all neutral pronouns would invariably become *he/ his/ him*. Of course, this isn't politically correct for the very politically correct world we live in nowadays.

Even though the singular *they* is commonly used when English is spoken, many people consider it to be grammatically incorrect. Surprisingly, there are a lot of people out there who care about this issue. Google lately came under fire because, within the Google+ social network, people are allowed to hide their gender, which prompts the use of *they* and *their* when updates are listed. Google's product manager even had to address the grammar issue in a video outlining the new privacy feature. Dennis Baron, a well-known grammarian and professor of English and Linguistics at the University of Chicago, has done extensive research into the lack of a gender-neutral pronoun. He cites numerous examples throughout history of attempts to coin a pronoun to replace the cumbersome coordinate *he or she*. Some of the suggested alternatives: *thon, his-her, le, ne, s/he,* and *ip*. Suffice it to say, all attempts have failed. So, how can a language with almost a million words not have a single word to address gender neutrality? This exemplifies one indisputable fact – English is **loco**. Don't worry; this word is now listed as being slang in English dictionaries.

So where does this leave English teachers? How do we teach students proper English? What's the difference between English being misused and English being incorrect? The truth is even many native speakers misuse English all the time. This is partly because, quite frequently, pop culture is viewed as a linguistic authority. Today kids are heard quoting Jay-Z more than Shakespeare, and they write shorthand text messages instead of full words. But what about other ways English is misused, which may not be as noticeable? For example, the word *decimation* is really meant to imply that ten percent of something is destroyed. However, it is commonly used as a synonym for destruction. The word *instant* really means an exact moment in time, although nowadays it is frequently used as meaning something that is prepared quickly. We use the words *less* and *fewer* when comparing quantities. *Fewer* is used with quantities that are countable, such as fewer apples, and *less* is used with quantities that are uncountable, such as less energy. But how often do you walk into a store and see a checkout lane that reads "10 items or less"? Since *items* are countable, why not correctly state "10 items or fewer"? Yet this begs a larger question. Is it okay for native English speakers to continue misusing their own language, even if it's incorrect?

Linguists, grammarians, and lexicographers of the English language might contend that without rules and standards to which language can adhere, communication would be encumbered. Basically, too much variance in English could mean two speakers of the language may not understand one another. Arguably, you could say this is happening today. Dialects between native English speakers of different geographical, generational, or economic backgrounds may sometimes have difficulty understanding one another due to nuances, slang, or colloquial expressions. It reminds me of the 1970s movie *Airplane*, when the little old white lady claimed that she spoke "Jive." This linguistic impasse ultimately impedes the basic purpose of learning a language, which is essentially to communicate.

In 2010, I witnessed firsthand a geographical variance of the English language when I traveled to Namibia. From the onset, I noticed English being used in a lot of unique ways. For starters, schoolchildren in Namibia are referred to as learners and not students. Only when someone attends university will they be called a student. Therefore, throughout this book, I've used the term learner. Also, Namibia has its linguistic roots primarily in British English, which is different for me since I'm American. This ultimately set a precedent for enunciation and spelling. But still, English in Namibia seems to be taking on a form of its own. I was constantly walking a tightrope of improper English and regional dialect. Some wording I found to be downright peculiar. Either way, my basic teaching instincts found it unacceptable, so I felt compelled to correct it. I tried but didn't succeed. My problem was that I believed people were using an erroneous form of English, while I spoke a standard form of the language. But maybe language has no limitations? Perhaps my real problem was the language was changing too fast for me to keep up, and I just wasn't able to realize this until I stepped out of my own environment.

My teaching experience in Namibia reminded me often of the serenity prayer: being granted the serenity to accept the things you cannot change, the courage to change the things you can, and wisdom to know the difference. There's no better place to see the value of education than in an undeveloped rural area. Opportunities are few and far between, which makes education incredibly vital. Obtaining an education is the first hurdle everyone must jump. And I came to Namibia hoping to give learners a boost over some of the obstacles that stand in their way.

While writing this book, I've tried to keep in mind an audience of prospective teachers who may consider going abroad. I write about some personal anecdotes in the classroom that may be applicable on a wider scale, but there's also a great deal of information specific to Namibia and teaching in a rural environment. Therefore, a person going to teach English in Hong Kong may not be able to relate to some of these experiences. Regardless, I've tried to inject humor when applicable, so I hope just about anyone may find my story amusing.

Watermelon is Life is the second part of my international teaching escapades, which I've illustrated in a series called *Do U English?* It's important to note that this book is entirely subjective, as no two experiences are alike. Other volunteer teachers in Namibia have completely different stories and opinions. But that is good because if a person goes abroad, they should want the experience to be completely their own. As for my experience, I've attempted to write about it openly, honestly, and to the best of my recollection. In attempting to capture my experience, I hope to shed some light on the life of a volunteer teacher in rural Namibia and perhaps inspire others to get involved, travel, and attempt to learn about other people and cultures. Only when stepping outside of our own environment can we catch a glimpse of the world in a different light.

With that, I will let you get on with it. For those who wish to express feedback, criticism, praise, or have questions about teaching abroad, please contact me via my website at www.WesWeston.com. Thanks for reading!

Chapter 1
The Call

"So what I'd like to know is…" The voice on the other end of the line paused. "…umm…" For some reason, she hesitated.

I was growing impatient as I paced back and forth in my living room. I had just prepared some pasta which was sitting in a bowl on the plastic table next to me.

"I would like to know if you would father my child." She spit out the sentence rapidly and with conviction. I stopped dead in my tracks, like prey catching wind of a nearby predator.

"Um…" was my initial response, followed by, "…err…" The tables had turned, and now I was hesitating. I didn't know what to say, so it seemed logical to pretend I didn't hear her in the first place.

"Can you hear me?" I spoke forcefully into my generic LG prepaid phone. "The reception isn't good! Can you repeat that?" This was actually a rare instance when my cell reception was crystal clear. I heard perfectly well what she had said. It just hadn't registered, or perhaps I wasn't allowing it to register.

She repeated the statement, but this time with more gusto. "I said…I WANT YOU TO FATHER MY CHILD."

My first thought – *Oh shit! She did just say what I thought she did.* I quickly jogged my memory for this woman's name. *Ah yes…Daniella.*

"Look…Daniella, I'm flattered, but do you really think that's a good idea?"

What are you saying? Is it a good idea? It's a horrible idea!

I was trying to be nice. I didn't know this woman well enough to be sarcastic with her, let alone father her child.

I had been living in rural Namibia for several months now and had a lot of new experiences under my belt. Thus far, my "out of the ordinary" Namibian highlights included:

1) Hitchhiking into town on a weekly basis. The cars were nearly as old as I was, had spare tires on just about every wheel, and were usually filled well beyond capacity with six or more occupants.

2) Watching donkeys and cattle graze outside my front door. Sometimes they would even get close enough to peek their head inside the house.

3) Enduring long intervals without running water. I had stockpiles of two-liter Coca-Cola bottles lined up on my kitchen counter. No shower refreshes you quite like holding a plastic bottle over your head.

4) Frequently losing electricity at night. However, I found candlelight rather soothing.

But this last request! *Ding, Ding, Ding, Ding!* We have a winner! Never have I been asked by a stranger to father a child. Unfortunately for her, the prize for providing me with my most unusual Namibian experience would not be a newborn baby. At least, I didn't think it would. Daniella still hadn't presented her case.

"I just think you would make a great father," she said. Her plan of attack – smooth talk! And I'm a sucker for compliments. It was a convincing argument, and a smile crossed my face when she said this.

Yes, you would make a great father.

"And you are such a handsome man," she continued.

Well, I've been blessed with a young face.

"I know the children would love you as if you were their real father."

What! She already has children?

We were getting our signals crossed. I decided to cut right to the chase. My parents always taught me to ask plenty of questions so you know what you're getting into.

"How many kids do you have?"

"I have two children. My baby boy is almost two years old and my little girl is eleven."

Gosh, that's a lot of responsibility.

"But don't worry about the girl. She is very responsible and takes good care of herself."

Daniella did have a point. Young children in rural areas of Namibia can be quite self-sufficient. They offer a lot of assistance in the home, and the help they provide is sometimes the impetus to have children in the first place. So why would she want a third child?

"If you already have two children, you really want to have a third with me?" I heard her giggle innocently on the other end of the line.

"No, I don't want another child right now. I'm looking for a father for my youngest child." I don't know why, but I was a little offended. Why **not** have a child with me? What did I do? What's wrong with me? This call was becoming more and more confusing.

"So you don't want to have another child with me?"

"NO!" she clearly stated. Now it sounded like she was the one who was worried. "But of course, we can talk about having another child." She tried to soften the blow.

Hmm…all talk and no play. This deal just keeps getting worse.

"I think one baby would be enough work right now," Daniella continued. "Taking care of two may be a little much for you."

Well, she's right about that. Two would be a little much. Best to start out with just one…WHAT THE HELL IS WRONG WITH YOU!

I'm not sure how I got caught up in the conversation, as though I may actually go through with this. First of all, I didn't even know Daniella. We had met just once before, and that was almost a month ago when a woman who looked to be in her late 20s approached me in the staffroom and introduced herself. She was a tall and slender woman with long braided hair which was likely extensions. Physically speaking, she was very attractive. However, when it comes to acting as a child's surrogate father, that kind of commitment is best made when you also know the mother's personality.

My initial encounter with Daniella was rather brief, and by brief I mean less than two minutes. She said she lived in the area and was enrolled in a college writing course. She asked if I would look at a paper she had written and check it for grammatical errors. I was more than willing to help a member of the community, so we exchanged phone numbers, and she told me she would be back the next day. She never returned. The next time I heard from her was when she made this phone call. I don't know how we went from editing a paper to fathering a child, but this was the jump we had made in our relationship. Of course, I do have a way with women!

"Daniella, I appreciate the offer. However, I don't think I'm father material just yet. "

"But a moment ago I thought you were asking if we'd have a baby."

"Yeah, I'm sorry. I got confused." I couldn't think of a good excuse so I blurted out, "The sun was in my eyes."

There was no response on the other end of the line. For a second, I thought she might have hung up, which would have been a relief because I had no idea how to end this call.

"Daniella, are you there?"

"Yes, I'm here," she responded.

Damn!

I decided I would try to appeal to her with simple logic and reason. She couldn't possibly think this would work. "To be honest,

I don't think this is a very good idea. Have you really thought this through?"

"Yes," she said confidently.

So much for logic and reason.

"Well, I don't think it would be possible," I said. "Actually, I know it won't be possible." I decided to end the call once and for all. "I really think that if you want to talk about this, we should have this conversation in person. I don't really feel comfortable talking about it over the phone." I think this was only fair, since certain social protocols – asking for a divorce, borrowing lots of money, inquiring if someone will be a child's surrogate father – are requests that are best presented face-to-face.

"I understand," she said. "I didn't think it would be something you'd be interested in."

Ah, guilt – the last resort. And it worked to some extent. I felt slightly culpable for depriving these children of a father figure, although I never did inquire about the status of their real father, or possibly fathers. But I was able to bite my tongue. I wasn't going to be guilted into fatherhood.

Daniella continued, "Next time I come by the school we can discuss this. Thank you for your time." With that, she hung up, and I immediately turned off my phone.

I walked over to the table and took a seat. For a moment, I drifted off into space and stared outside. I watched as a drove of donkeys meandered by my house heading for the front gate of the school. I could see the silhouette of many learners sitting on concrete benches under the shade of trees. Finally, remembering that I hadn't eaten lunch, I learned forward and grabbed my bowl of lukewarm pasta.

Chapter 2
Invasion of the Oshilumbu

I was exhausted by the time we arrived at Eengedjo Senior Secondary School. A swing gate opened up onto the property, and there was a concrete wall on each side of it. On the left wall, there was an illustration of two golden bells with the name of the school written above. Later, I would learn that in the local dialect, *Eengedjo* is the word for *bell*. Below the two bells was an inscription that read "Knowledge is Strength" – the school's motto. On the wall to the right of the gate was a painting of Namibia's coat of arms. It showed two orxy, which is a large species of antelope, standing on either side of a blue, green, and red shield, the Namibian colors. I had time to take notice of such details because the security guard manning the gate was inexplicably absent.

Eventually, one of the learners approached the gate with a set of keys. Once the lock was removed, the gates swung open. The driver put the truck in gear, and we rolled onto the dusty school grounds. Suddenly, all the eyes of Eengedjo were upon me.

It immediately became evident just how far I was outside of my natural environment. In a way, I felt trapped, both physically and metaphorically. To keep me in, there was a fence that ran along the perimeter of the school, a mild security measure. Besides, outside of these walls there was nowhere to go, no escape. There were just farms, barren lands, and tiny villages. For better or for worse, I would inhabit the grounds of Eengedjo for an entire school year.

When we drove onto the property, I knew what it felt like to be an animal on display at a zoo. All eyes were fixed on me with a mixture of curiosity and bewilderment. Hundreds of learners were loitering around outside. Most were huddled in groups, standing under various acacia trees located at the front of the school. The trees were not very tall, and their branches extended outward over the earth at about the height of a person. The foliage of the tree offered blissful shade from the brutal sun. It's as if the universe specifically designed these trees for people to congregate under. Even though it was late in the afternoon, most of the learners were still dressed in their school uniforms. The boys wore a white, button-up shirt with black slacks and shoes. The girls wore the same white shirt but with black skirts. Everyone gazed at the truck as we drove slowly around the school looking for the security guard who held the keys to my flat. The anxiety I was giving off was palpable.

"I think they are looking at you," the driver said with a smile.

Of course they're looking at me. I'm the only white guy in this village.

Jokingly, I told him, "I don't know. They may be looking at you." The driver was a man in his 50s who worked for the Ministry of Education (MOE). He had a large nose and a lighter skin color than the learners of Eengedjo. He told me he was Herero, one of several ancestral tribes that reside in Namibia. However, at the time, I had not considered the unique differences among the various ethnic groups. I told him, "Maybe they've never seen a Herero person before."

The driver chuckled. "Nah, I'm pretty sure they are looking at you." I forced a smile, but all I could really focus on was the brick of apprehension in my stomach.

We eventually hit a dead end, and the driver asked one of the learners the whereabouts of the security guard. The kid pointed back in the direction from which we came, so we turned the truck around for another victory lap. Usually, I enjoy getting attention, but as we idled across the school grounds, I was daunted by the eyes of

Eengedjo. I looked down at the turtle sitting on the floorboard between my feet and thought how fortunate he was. He could shrivel up into his shell and escape from the world at will. However, I stopped envying the turtle when I remembered he would be dinner later that evening.

I was determined not to hide from my onlookers like a frightened turtle, so I looked back at them and smiled, equally curious about the experience we were getting ready to share together. I had to remind myself that this is what I wanted. I sought to embrace this change and uncertainty, even if it aroused a melting pot of feelings ranging from angst to adrenaline. A lot of people tend to shy away from change and become complacent with the rigors of monotony. Therefore, I tried to appreciate the beauty of my situation because moments like this don't happen often in life. I had been taken far off course and could think of no greater change in my life than living in the African bush of rural Namibia.

As we made our way back to the front of the school, some of the learners pointed us in the right direction. Soon we found an old man standing in front of a nondescript white house. The security guard held up a set of keys as the truck rolled to a stop in front of him. I was home.

The day began 10 hours earlier in the capital city of Windhoek. Nowadays, when people hear the word "capital," they generally tend to picture a bustling metropolis with congested roads, crowded sidewalks, and pollution you can almost taste. If anything, Namibia is a land of perspective, and the country gives a whole new meaning to the expression, "Everything is relative." In terms of land area, Namibia is the 34th largest country in the world, roughly twice the size of the state of California. What the country does NOT have is people. Namibia has a population of just over 2.1 million people,

Entering the front gate of Eengedjo Senior Secondary School

which gives it the 2nd lowest population density in the world. This ultimately means the bustling metropolis of Windhoek is neither bustling nor a metropolis. It has a population of fewer than 350,000 residents, and by some countries' standards, this capital is merely a small town.

Our group of volunteers left that small town in separate vehicles on a Monday morning. Our transport was provided by the MOE, and I accompanied six other volunteers whose teaching placements were also in the northern region of the country. Early that morning, after saying goodbye to some of the other volunteers whose teaching placements were elsewhere, we were off. The only stop we made was for lunch, except for a minor holdup to pick up a turtle that was in the middle of the road. At first, I thought it magnanimous of the driver to stop and help the little fellow. But when the driver brought the turtle back to the car, I became curious. The turtle was going to make a fine meal for the driver and his family. I had never eaten turtle, and I guess I'm not opposed to trying it. But this got me thinking about all of the exotic foods I might try over the course of the coming year.

The ride north was scenic. Geographically, Namibia is mostly desert land. We drove across a barren landscape with little vegetation and grasslands that looked thirsty for water. Contrary to what one might think, the land appeared quite vibrant. Its soft colors and the occasional wild boar on the side of the road animated the desolate countryside.

Early in the afternoon, we arrived in the town of Ondangwa, the MOE's northern headquarters. Our separation was abrupt, and there was a flurry of emotional goodbyes as we each went our separate way. Our group of volunteers had grown close during the three weeks of orientation, and I had no idea when I would see them again. From there, I continued on with the same driver who had driven us from Windhoek. Soon, I would reach my new home. At least, that's what I thought.

The driver, the turtle, and I left Ondangwa at 3 p.m. My village was only 50 kilometers away, and since there is absolutely NO traffic in Namibia, it should have taken about a half hour. I figured I would get there with plenty of daylight. However, during this second leg of the journey, we embarked on a cultural scenic route. First, we stopped to get gas – *Okay, that's understandable.* Then we skipped over to KFC, which is surprisingly plentiful throughout Namibia, so the driver could get some food – *Sure, everyone has to eat.* After, we dropped off boxes of paper at a church retreat – *It's fine. I'm flexible.* Then, the driver informed me we were going to pick up another teacher who needed a lift to a village that was on our way – *Well, I guess.*

We stopped at a petrol station where we were supposed to meet this woman. The driver got out and chatted up someone in the parking lot – seems like everyone in Namibia knows each other – while the turtle and I waited patiently in the car. Thirty minutes rolled by and the woman was still hadn't show up. I was getting tired of waiting. Even the turtle looked like he was getting restless. At this point it was 4:30 p.m. We left an hour and a half ago and had covered only about 20 kilometers. Finally, the lady arrived, and the driver, the teacher, the turtle, and I crammed onto the bench seat of the pickup. Without any further delays, our journey came to an end at 4:55 p.m. with our triumphant arrival at my new home of Omungwelume.

Omungwelume, as legend has it, is supposedly named after a huge male tiger that lived in the area before people settled there. Of course, tigers are not a species from Africa, so this is just a myth. What was true, at least for me, was the difficulty enunciating Omungwelume because it is not pronounced the way it is spelled. Everyone in Omungwelume pronounced it *Ohm-gway-loo-may*. Since I had a natural tendency to say it like it was spelled [*Oh-mung-way-loo-may*], even adding an extra syllable, I misspoke on numerous occasions, and each time I was corrected by a colleague or learner until I eventually got it right. It made me sympathize with the learners since the English language is masterful for having words pronounced differently from the way they are spelled.

Home to just over a thousand residents, Omungwelume, in many respects, is just a village. However, a colleague who is from there tried to convince me it is in fact a town. Apparently, Omungwelume had ascended into township in 2009 after being upgraded from a village. I have no idea who made this assessment and with what criteria, but my colleague seemed quite proud of his "town's" achievement. Therefore, I saw no need to question his claim. Yet my own eyes told a different story.

When we arrived in Omungwelume, there was only one paved road that went right through town, and to envision how far commerce stretched along this road, I could probably throw a rock from one end to the other. Well, maybe not a rock, but one of those long-distance Frisbees. Nevertheless, the main drag of Omungwelume boasted a couple of mini-marts where basic food stuff could be bought, two hairdressers, a bakery, a photo studio, and several small stores referred to as "China shops." These shops are generic retail stores that sell just about anything, and they can be found all over the country. All the products are made in China, and the proprietors are – you guessed it – Chinese. But by far the most dominant business enterprise in Omungwelume were *shabeens*. A shabeen is a small bar that primarily sells beer and cigarettes, but many also carry rum, whiskey, and bourbon. Their numbers are superfluous throughout Namibia, and even little Omungwelume had about a half dozen shabeens.

In order to visualize "downtown" Omungwelume, imagine all those stores and businesses I just mentioned. Now put them in small, concrete block buildings with basic electricity and often no plumbing. An outside décor was painted on only about half of the buildings. Many were just labeled with an ordinary name stating their business, like "Shop" or "Hairdresser." Upon first seeing these places, it made me wonder about the legality behind such an enterprise. It almost seemed that to be an entrepreneur, all one really needed was a concrete building and a can of paint to write a name on the outside.

As we drove through Omungwelume, which took all of five seconds, I wasn't sure what to make of it. To the untrained eye, Omungwelume didn't have much. And upon first glance, the place sure did look like a village. However, Omungwelume was a happening place compared to…well, absolutely nothing. Once again, everything is relative. I guess when someone has to come to Omungwelume to pick up supplies, that's when a person knows they live in a village.

The driver turned off the main road and onto a small dirt road. We passed by concrete houses irregularly placed on small plots of land, until suddenly we were forced to stop. Several cattle were crossing the road in front of us. The driver said it was getting late, so the cattle should be going home.

Do cows in Namibia know they have a curfew?

Just after he made the comment, a little boy walked up behind the last straggler, a cow about ten times his size, and prodded it with a stick. The boy was shirtless and without shoes, wearing just a pair of worn-torn blue jeans. As we passed him, he glared at me and muttered the word, "Oshilumbu."

Oshilumbu literally means *white person*. North-central Namibia is heavily dominated by the Ovambo tribe, whose people have a dark skin color. Thus, I stood out no less than a black sheep. The Ovambo tribe is the country's largest ethnic group and is spread primarily across northern Namibia and southern Angola. They are part of the Bantu family, whose African origins date back thousands of years. The Ovambo people speak a language called Oshiwambo, of which there are many different dialects. For example, where I lived the people spoke Oshikwanyama. *Oshilumbu* is a word from Oshiwambo, and I think it's universal among all the dialects since I would hear it just about everywhere.

Once the cattle had passed, we carried on, and eventually the dirt road led us to the front gates of Eengedjo. I could not have been more relieved because I was exhausted after a long day of travel, but I was home. As I unloaded my luggage from the back of the truck, it was surreal to think I would be unpacking these bags for the first time in weeks.

When I opened the front door to the house, I saw a giant long-legged spider scurry across the floor and onto a wall. He joined over a dozen other little spiders that appeared stuck on the walls like stickers. I paid little attention to the small arachnids and dragged my luggage through the door. The house hadn't been occupied in over a month, and a thick coat of dust had already settled on the floor. Yet the place looked pleasant enough. All things considered, it was actually a very nice residence. There was a large open living room that contained a plastic table, two chairs, and a shelving unit cluttered with books, magazines, and administration files. There was also a mini-refrigerator in the corner, although it was broken. The walls were sparsely decorated with magazine clippings, maps of Namibia, and several welcome signs the local kids had made for me. They had written messages like:

Welcome Mr. Wes. May God Bless U!
Welcome to Omungwelume. I wish good life.
Welcome to Namibia. Feel at home to be in Namibia.

I don't know the ages of the kids who wrote the signs, and some didn't even write their names. However, I imagine the school's previous volunteer prompted this activity. And it worked! I felt at home as soon as I walked in the door.

My eyes eventually moved beyond the front living room and I noticed the kitchen was straight back. By design, these rooms were shared spaces since each side of the house was a separate unit. It was basically a duplex, and each unit had two bedrooms and a bathroom. For a single occupant in rural Namibia, I had hit the jackpot of living space.

Shortly after I arrived, the principal of the school walked over to greet me. He was a tall, amiable man in his 40s, and he came right in to introduce himself. "Hello. You must be Mr. Wes!" he said cheerfully. "I am Mr. Joseph."

Throughout Namibia, personal titles such as Mr. or Miss are often used with a person's first name. Mr. Joseph immediately shook my hand. In orientation, we learned about different greetings and introductions. The handshake, for example, consists of three consecutive movements. First, grasp the other person's hand as with any normal handshake. Next, both people momentarily move their hands into a position as though they're locking in an arm wrestle. Finally, the hand returns to the initial handshake position. When shaking hands like this, it made me feel like I belonged to a club. The principal immediately took notice of my etiquette.

"Mr. Wes, you're Namibian already," he said and patted me on the back.

Mr. Joseph gave me a quick tour of the house. He showed me around and pointed out some of its amenities, as well as some of the improvements he wanted to make. For example, I was missing a stove for cooking, but one was brought to me by the end of the week. Since I was the only volunteer in the area, I would have the place to myself and would occupy the unit on one side of the house. Curious, I walked over to the closed door leading to the other unit and Mr. Joseph quickly stopped me.

"This door stays shut all the time," he said.

The way he said it invoked my curiosity. "What's over there?" I asked.

"There's nothing good over there, Mr. Wes," the principal said in a solemn tone. "I wouldn't worry about it," he assured me.

But the way he said it, I **did** worry, like there may be a tomb or perhaps that side of the house was hexed with an evil spirit. Maybe I would be opening Eengedjo's very own *Chamber of Secrets*. After that cautionary warning, the principal bade me goodnight. I would see him at the school's daily staff meeting the next morning, which he said began promptly at 6:40 a.m.

As tired as I was at the end of the day, my nerves kept me from getting much sleep. My mind was flush with activity about my first day of school. I thought about all the kids I was going to teach and the people I would meet throughout the year. My skin color alone assured I would make a big first impression. What I didn't know is that I would sound the alarm throughout all of Omungwelume that the *oshilumbu* had arrived.

Chapter 3
Air Raid

My alarm sounded at 6:05 a.m.

This is WAY too early.

As I rolled over to face the window, I could barely discern a faint hint of sunlight creeping into the room. I had an entire year of getting up with the sun to look forward to. I dragged myself out of bed and jumped into a cold shower, which shocked some life into me. Then I got dressed, grabbed my backpack full of pens, pencils, and notebooks, and walked out the door.

The staff room was located in the main building, only 50 meters from my house. It was an old building constructed in 1975, and apart from the occasional paint job, it appeared there had been few renovations. I attempted to walk to the building surreptitiously, but it was to no avail. Many of the learners were already outside, standing around in groups waiting for the bell to ring. The kids eyed me curiously, much like the day before. When I passed by the first group of learners, I flashed them a smile.

"Good morning, Mr. Oshilumbu," a boy proclaimed in a jovial manner. The other kids smiled. I told them good morning, waved hello, and continued walking since I didn't want to be late to my first staff meeting. Along the way, I received another salutation to which I was unaccustomed.

"Good morning, sir," said a girl as I walked by. I wasn't sure how I felt about being called *sir*. To me, it seemed a bit formal and made me feel old. But such titles are common, so for the most part my new names would be *Sir* or *Mr. Wes*. On occasion, I would get *Master Wes*, which really sounded weird.

I entered the staffroom from the back of the building. It was half past six, and most of the teachers were already there. The staffroom was a large space with six long wooden tables positioned in the shape of a horseshoe. The tables were littered with huge stacks of papers, notebooks, binders, and textbooks. It looked like a bomb of school bureaucracy had just exploded. The teachers had designated spaces where they did their work, and when I entered, Mr. Joseph immediately showed me to an empty chair.

The principal then kicked off the staff meeting with my introduction. I was so nervous I don't even remember what I said, but I vaguely recall trying to open with a joke. What I do remember is my words being followed by an awkward applause. Then, going around the room one by one, the other staff members introduced themselves, stating their name and the subject they taught. Afterwards, the spotlight went back on the principal as he began discussing a new memo from the MOE. As soon as the meeting adjourned, I was handed my class schedule for the week.

What the heck is this!

I had to forget about the traditional Monday through Friday school schedule and think of it in terms of days. The days were listed from 1 to 7, presumably to correspond with the number of days in a week. During the school day, regular class hours were from 7:00 a.m. till 12:45 p.m., which consisted of seven classes that were 45 minutes each. At 10 o'clock there was a 30-minute break for everyone. My first day at Eengedjo was on a Tuesday, but since school officially started the week before, according to our schedule it was Day 7. The next day, Wednesday, would then start over at Day 1. Therefore, it was important to know which day in the schedule we were on. Suffice it to say, this made lesson planning rather cumbersome in the beginning.

Luckily, my very first class on Day 7 was an administration period. This time was intended for teachers to plan lessons or mark papers, although some teachers seemed to use administration periods for downtime since our staffroom had a television that was usually turned to some ridiculous Mexican soap soap opera.[1] After the administration period, I was going to teach six classes in a row until the end of the day. It was nice to have the first 45 minutes to mentally prepare. However, I spent the first half of the period unproductively looking at the clock, counting down the minutes until show time. The longer I waited, the more anxious I became. What would the kids think of me? Will they like me as a teacher? I needed something to occupy my mind, so I decided to have a look at the computer room.

Apart from teaching English and math, I would also teach computer skills to all the grade 12 classes. I wanted to have a look at the setup, especially since I had been forewarned by the previous volunteer not to expect much. He told me the computers were old and outdated. I really just wanted to see if the machines would boot up.

The school's computer room was located just outside of the staffroom. The principal pointed it out the day before when he presented me with a set of keys, which included a house key, a staffroom key, and the key to the computer room. I walked outside and over to a large, corrugated metal door secured shut with a heavy duty padlock. I put the key in, turned it to its side, and the lock released. I felt a sense of pride. Here I was, already entrusted with one of the school's valuable resources. I had my own computer room. A smile crossed my face.

---

[1] These soap operas, which are dubbed in English, are extremely popular. They are played repeatedly over the Namibian Broadcasting Channel (NBC). When I was in Namibia, the most popular TV show was Pasión de Gavilones (Passion of Hawks). It was a monster hit.

As I pushed open the door, I was hit with a jolt of panic. Sirens started blaring, putting even the loudest blow horns to shame. It sounded like a full-on civil defense siren, which everyone in Omungwelume could probably hear. Were there bombers overhead? Was there a fire? Had we entered into a state of national emergency? In the end, it was just the resident *oshilumbu* breaking into the computer room. I opened the door and looked inside. There was a keypad mounted on the wall next to the door, and I remembered Mr. Joseph telling me something about a passcode.

Oh yeah, the school still needs to give me one. Crap! I can't turn this thing off!

Some of the learners peeked out of the classroom to see what the commotion was all about. Even a few of the teachers walked outside. I had disrupted the very first class of the day. All I could do was wave to my audience.

That's right everyone! There'll be another show later. Don't worry. I'll be here all year!

Some of the kids waved to me as the teachers ushered them back inside the rooms. Eventually, Mr. Joseph came to my rescue. But suddenly, another teacher caught his attention from behind and the two conversed for a moment while I stood there waiting. Even from a few feet away, I couldn't hear their conversation. For a siren that conveyed such a high state of emergency, there didn't seem to be a sense of urgency to turn it off. Finally, the principal came over and typed in a code that disarmed the system.

I thought he might be annoyed at the disturbance, but he had a big grin on his face. "You like our alarm system, Mr. Wes? It's very good! Very loud!" he stated with a proud and passionate fist pump.

"Yeah, I don't think anyone has difficulty hearing it," I told him, and then apologized for the disruption.

"Don't worry," he reassured me. "It's a very good system. The only problem is that it goes off all the time."

The principal showed me his six-digit code and said I could use it until they assigned me one. He then returned to the staffroom, and the remaining learners filed back into their classrooms. The spectacle was over. It's always good to make a first impression, but this was not what I had in mind. I had made my presence felt. If the people of Omungwelume didn't already know I was here, they did now.

Chapter 4

It's Not WHAT you Know, It's WHOM you Know

Namibia is a small country. I'll say that again. Namibia is a small country. I think most people are familiar with the concept of the small-town mentality. Information spreads like wildfire and everyone knows just about everyone else's business. You sneeze, and someone on the other end of town says, "Bless you." But this really can't apply to Namibia since the cultural norm is to not say anything after a person sneezes. Namibia is also not a town, but a country. Still, if there's a country version of this analogy then that's Namibia. And if Namibia were to be broken down by regions, then it becomes even more evident. You know EVERYONE.

Even though a lot of Namibians know each other, not many outsiders know of Namibia. So why is Namibia relatively unknown? Well, for starters it's a very young country. Namibia achieved its independence in 1990, and when I was there the country was getting ready to celebrate its 20th anniversary. I think it's only fair to do Namibia a bit of justice with some historical context, so here's a brief lesson.

In post-colonial times, Namibia was occupied by several different groups of people. In the north, there were the Ovambo and Kavango ethnic groups, both decedents of the Bantu nation and predominantly farmers who also traded metal goods. In the grasslands of central Namibia were the Damara people, who arrived in the 9ᵗʰ century, and settled in an area which suitably became known as Damaraland. Farther south was a group known as the Nama who settled around the Orange River, which serves as the present-day border between Namibia and South Africa. In the 17ᵗʰ century, a pastoral nomadic group called the Herero entered Namibia and clashed with the Nama over control of the land. Then in the 19ᵗʰ century, white farmers known as the Orlams, entered from the south and began settling across the Orange River. The Orlams, who were descendants of the Boers and spoke Afrikaans, began vying for land with both the Nama and Herero. These groups didn't live together harmoniously, and competition for land remained fierce.

The first Europeans to step foot on Namibian soil were the Portuguese in 1485. However, it wasn't until the 19ᵗʰ century that Europe began taking a stronger interest in the territory. After colonization got underway, Namibia became a German colony in 1884. In the early 1900s, both the Nama and Herero people took up arms against the Germans, which resulted in the Herero and Nama genocide. Around 10,000 Nama (half the population) and 65,000 Herero (80% of the population) were killed. After Germany was defeated in World War I, the colony was then occupied by South Africa as part of a mandate by the League of Nations. The territory became part of South Africa and was known as South-West Africa. After World War II, the League of Nations was replaced with the United Nations (UN), which rescinded the original mandate and required that Namibia come under UN supervision. However, South Africa refused to surrender its authority. Thus, the struggle for independence began.

The most well-known group of freedom fighters throughout Namibia was the South-West Africa People's Organization (SWAPO). In the mid-1960s, SWAPO began planning guerrilla attacks against South Africa in an effort for liberation. International pressure was put on South Africa, but throughout the 1970s and 1980s the message from global powers such as the United States was unclear. The liberty and independence of African nations became muddled with stopping the spread of Communism. Namibia fell between the pro-U.S. South Africa and the Soviet-Cuban influence of Angola. Over the years, negotiations between political party leaders of Namibia and South Africa – many of which excluded SWAPO – made little progress. Therefore, Namibia continued to be administered by South Africa and its policies of apartheid.

Finally, in 1988, a mediation team headed by the United States brought Angola, Cuba, and South Africa into negotiations, and in December of 1988, an agreement was reached that South Africa would hand control of Namibia over to the UN. The nearly year-long government transition was relatively smooth. South Africa withdrew its forces, political prisoners were granted amnesty, and discriminatory legislation was repealed. Elections were held the following year, and SWAPO took 57% of the vote. Namibia officially became an independent nation on March 21, 1990, and the country's first president, Sam Nujoma, was sworn into office.

Sam Nujoma is perhaps the most famous person in Namibia. Even before independence, he had been the president of SWAPO and a long-time champion of freedom. Nujoma secured the presidency due to his immense popularity, which also helped him get re-elected in 1994 and once again in 1999. This then concluded his constitutional right to run for a fourth-term. With the country still under the strong influence of SWAPO, Sam Nujoma's handpicked successor, Hifikepunye Pohamba, was elected president in 2004. Pohamba was still in office, serving his second term, when I arrived in 2010.

Namibia is not just a country with a rich and turbulent history, but it is also home to some of the most spectacular geography on the planet. The Namib Desert is composed of five-million-year-old sand and has some of the highest sand dunes in the world, standing at over 300 meters high. Fish River Canyon, located in the south of Namibia, is the second largest canyon in the world next to the Grand Canyon.

Although the country is arid and may appear somewhat inhospitable, there is an abundance of wildlife that calls Namibia home. Etosha National Park is one of the premiere game reserves in Southern Africa. It has over 20,000 km² of protected land, and the park is a melting pot of African wildlife. People can encounter exotic animals, such as lions, elephants, giraffes, zebras, rhinoceros, wildebeest, hyenas, and the adorable dikdik, which is a small antelope that looks like a miniature deer. And it's Namibia's wildlife inhabitants that truly complement the country's natural splendor.

All of Namibia's beauty is contained in a land area of 825,418 km². This is a relatively large space compared to its modest population of 2.1 million people. Given Namibia's geographical size to human population, the country's development is on a small scale. It doesn't necessarily take long to see much of the inhabited areas. Therefore, in many respects, Namibia is a very small country. But let me put it this way – every time I look at pictures from Namibia on the Internet, I feel like it's a street I have previously been on or an exact location I have already visited. For three years, I lived in South Korea, which is roughly *1/8* of Namibia's geographical size. However, Korea is *25 times* more populated than Namibia and much more developed. In the one year I spent in Namibia, it feels as if I have seen much more of the country than I did of South Korea in the three years I spent there. It's no wonder that Namibia is sort of a village within itself.

Shortly after alerting everyone of my presence with the alarm fiasco, I was getting ready to take center stage. My first class was about to start, and another teacher pointed me in the direction of my classroom. I grabbed my backpack, hoisted it on my shoulders, and marched out the door.

The layout of the school's buildings formed a rectangle, but one with only three sides which were not actually connected. The short side of this rectangle was the main building where the staffroom was located. Stretching out from the back of the main building – the long sides of the rectangle – were the classrooms. On either side, there were three separate concrete buildings, which contained four classrooms each and faced one another across a large courtyard. The center pieces of this design were several large marula trees standing proudly in the middle of the courtyard. Directly across from the main building, at the far end of the courtyard, was an open space, but a short ways beyond were three more buildings – a dining hall, a boys' dormitory, and a girls' dormitory.

Eengedjo Senior Secondary School had just over 700 learners, and the school contained grades 8 to 12, even though grades 8, 9, and 10 were technically part of junior secondary school. However, the reason Eengedjo was considered a senior secondary school is because the vast majority of learners were in grades 11 and 12. At Eengedjo, there were six classes of grade 12 and seven classes of grade 11, compared to two classes each of grades 8, 9, and 10. All classes were differentiated alphabetically, so the seven grade 11 classes were given letters A to G. Each class was fixed; therefore, the learners would have all of their subjects within their assigned classroom while the teachers rotated.

After leaving the staffroom, I raced across the courtyard at a brisk urban pace, still far from acclimating to the deliberate slowness of rural living. My very first class was an English class with grade 11C, and during the course of the year, I would teach English to two grade 11 classes. I was also going to teach a grade 9 math class, computer skills to all grade 12 classes, and a class called business information systems to grades 8, 9, and 10. Fortunately, my schedule permitted me to teach many of the classes at Eengedjo, so I got to interact with most of the learners.

When I reached the 11C classroom, I immediately noticed that it was missing a door. In fact, many of the school's classrooms were without doors. They had either been taken off, had fallen off, or were ripped off. Windows were in a similar state of dilapidation, and many were either broken or missing. I paused momentarily just outside the room, listening to the mirthful clamor of the learners. I tried to soak in this momentous occasion. Everything had been leading up to this point, and in many ways, the year was about to officially begin.

Meeting a new class of students is kind of like being on a blind date. Act pleasantly surprised at the beginning, don't try to move too fast, and leave them wanting more. I walked up the steps leading to the classroom and stood in the doorway. Slowly, heads began to turn my way, and there was a swift hush over the learners. They were all dressed neatly in their school uniforms, and many of them had a smile on their faces.

I entered the room, and in a loud, cheerful voice said, "GOOD MORNING!" Some of the learners giggled at my exuberance.

Almost in unison, the class replied, "Good morning, sir!"

Suddenly, they began to stand up from their chairs, which is tradition whenever the teacher enters the classroom. But like many traditions, it's not always practiced, and in some ways, the custom is starting to disappear. Since this was our first class together, I'm sure the learners wanted to make a good impression. Once everyone was standing, I noticed the disproportionate learner to chair ratio. And when I told them to take a seat, I watched as several learners crammed onto a single chair with another classmate.

Everyone stared at me with a look suggesting, *"What's this crazy oshilumbu going to do next."* On the surface, our greatest difference would appear to be based on skin color, but this really wasn't the case. The tone of our class was going to be set on our experiences. I had never taught in an area as rural as Omungwelume, and this factor certainly influenced the classroom environment. For their part, I don't believe they had ever had a foreign teacher and been exposed to different teaching methodologies. Many of the learners in this class were new to Eengedjo, which meant they would not have met the previous volunteer. But our diversity was a positive attribute. It meant that we were all eager to learn.

I introduced myself to the learners as Mr. Wes and wrote my name on the chalkboard. I then told them we would formally begin our lessons at the end of the week. First, I wanted to get to know them. I had numerous ideas for icebreakers and fun games. But before we jumped into those activities, I asked the learners if they had any questions for me. A learner in the back of the classroom raised his hand. I acknowledged the boy's question and asked him to state his name.

"My name is Hango," the boy said. In Namibia, *Hango* is a popular name, although it's actually a surname. Hango was short in stature and his shaved head accentuated his rounded face. His smile exuded a positive energy, and he carried an expression that he was about to say something funny before he even spoke.

"Mr. Wes, do you know Beyoncé?" Some of the other learners laughed, and I immediately pegged Hango as the class clown. Even though he was smiling, he maintained a hopeful disposition, as if he expected I might say yes. In fact, all the learners had a look of anticipation.

I sarcastically responded, "Of course I know Beyoncé." The learners' expression changed to excitement and many of their eyes lit up. Apparently, even in rural Namibia, Beyoncé is quite famous. Then I started to push the envelope. "Actually, if you must know the truth," I told them. "She's my ex-girlfriend."

I maintained a serious temperament to play along with this little joke. There was a mix of reactions among the learners. Some learners appeared excited at the prospect that I used to date Beyoncé, while others who seemed skeptical had a convincing argument.

"No, this is not true. Sir, Beyoncé would not like you."

"Why is that?" I asked them. "Because I'm an oshilumbu?" The classroom erupted with laughter. The kids loved that I was already starting to pick up their native language of Oshikwanyama.

"Beyoncé likes Jay-Z," they assured me. I cringed at the very mention of his name.

"Wow, don't even get me started on that guy," I told them. "Talk about the biggest mistake she's ever made. She left me…for him! Can you believe it?"

"Yes, Jay-Z is very rich," a learner shouted from the side of the room. For an isolated area thinly connected by slow Internet speeds, the kids certainly seemed up to date on some of the latest pop culture news from the U.S.

I bantered with the class in this manner for a while, but I forgot to mention I was kidding. I kind of assumed it was easy to pick up on my sarcasm, not taking into account that in some cultures sarcasm is seldom used. Eventually, I segued into an activity, and it was no longer discussed.

My other classes that day went more or less the same way. Only after the day was over did I recognize a pattern. When I asked the learners if they had questions for me, they always inquired if I personally knew some iconic figure. As they kept grilling me with more detailed questions about celebrities I had dated or befriended, I continued to joke with them, unaware that some of them actually believed me.

"Do you know Shakira?" – She's another ex-girlfriend.

"Do you know Barack Obama?" – We attended the same church in Chicago.

"Do you know Lil Wayne?" – He sat behind me in math class and would always copy my exams.

The next day I was forced to come clean and confessed that I had never met any of these people. The kids didn't really seem disappointed but rather confused. Many of them asked, "Why not?"

America is a big country that dwarfs Namibia in terms of geographical size and population. I don't think the learners were able to grasp the enormity of this difference. When I asked the learners if they knew famous people in Namibia, some of them said yes. It wasn't that uncommon to meet pop stars or important political figures. Then I thought back to my first week of orientation when the volunteers did an overnight host stay with local Namibians. A couple of volunteers stayed with the country's most famous female musical artists, Gal Level. Of course, nobody in our group knew who they were. But since the program coordinator's husband was a musician, he set it up. It made me realize that I wasn't able to see things from their perspective any more than they could comprehend mine.

I told the learners the only famous person I had ever met was the late Sam Walton, founder of the retail giant Wal-Mart. However, the learners showed no enthusiasm for my claim to have met the multi-billionaire. Even though at the time of his death, in 1992, Sam Walton's net worth was roughly *10 times* greater than Namibia's entire Gross Domestic Product. Yet I refrained from discussing Sam Walton's wealth since it would only exacerbate the perceived notion that all Americans are filthy rich. Truth is, I didn't have to bring it up because I was automatically being pinned as the Sam Walton of Omungwelume.

Over time I grew accustomed to this small community-like country. When I would travel to the larger town of Oshakati, and by large I mean a population of just over 30,000 people, I would start to recognize certain individuals. And even if I didn't, they certainly remembered me. I wasn't used to such recognition because I had always lived in areas where you could retain complete anonymity while walking the streets. Everywhere I went, especially around Omungwelume, I was constantly greeting people and saying hello. Granted, this was normal because greetings are an important aspect of Ovambo culture. But slowly, I was beginning to realize just how small Namibia really is.

I think it all came to a head a few months after I arrived. I checked my Facebook account one day and saw that I had received a friend request from Sam Nujoma, the first president of Namibia. At the time, I had been receiving numerous requests from people whom I didn't know. Social networks in Namibia were starting to take shape as more and more people were accessing the Internet for the first time. Just out of curiosity I went to Sam Nujoma's homepage, and from the minimal amount of information I could see – because we weren't "friends" – it looked like his actual account. However, other people may have been administering it for him. Now when it comes to Facebook, I don't typically add everyone who throws a friend request my way. Although I knew a great deal about Sam Nujoma, I didn't actually know the man. Perhaps part of me regrets it, but I ignored his request.

Chapter 5

Great Expectations

My second day at Eengedjo, once classes had ended, there was a knock at my door. When I opened it, there was a group of boys standing in front of me.

After we exchanged pleasantries, one of the older boys prodded a younger one standing in front. The boys had come to my house for a reason. Eventually, the young boy spoke up.

"Sir, we wonder if you will open the computer room today. Last year, Mr. Chris opened the room for us."

Ah, technology. These kids are thirsty for the world of computers.

Who could blame them since they never had the opportunity to use a computer at home? They really just wanted to play games, and when I was a kid I was no different. I had spent hours in front of my old-school Nintendo playing *Super Mario Bros., Contra,* and *The Legend of Zelda.*

At the time, however, it wasn't possible for them to use the computers. When I checked them the day before, I couldn't get most of them to turn on. And since I was entrusted with the computer room, Information Technology (IT) was supposedly my field of expertise. If anyone was going to get the computers functioning, it would have to be me. I told the kids I needed a little more time, but once I got the computers up and running the room would be open for business.

Later that day, two more learners knocked on my door. This time it was a boy and a girl from Grade 12. They introduced themselves as the Head Boy and Head Girl of Eengedjo, which meant they were the student body presidents. After we talked briefly, they arrived at the point of their visit.

"Sir, are you going to show us a movie this weekend?" asked the Head Boy, Eros. "Mr. Chris would always show us movies." I told them that showing movies was a tradition I definitely wanted to carry on. However, I still needed to figure out the process, like who to ask for permission and where to get the projector. I said I would look into it for the coming weekend but couldn't make any promises. I had already been in touch with Mr. Chris via email, and he had given me a rundown of activities he was involved in. I hadn't realized the kids would expect me to pick up right where he left off. I ignorantly assumed I would be given ample time to adjust to my new environment and not be bombarded with questions. Apparently, the time I was being allotted was ONE DAY.

Before they left, Eros left me with one last gem of information. "Sir, just so you know. Everyone loves *Harry Potter*."

Mr. Chris had told me that he had shown the first two movies in the series, and they were a tremendous hit. I nodded in agreement, but I guess Eros felt that I hadn't completely understood the magnitude of the learners' affection for the young wizard. "I'm serious, sir. Everyone **loves** *Harry Potter*."

Over the next couple of days, many of the kids made the same requests, along with some others.

"Sir, when are you going to open the computer room?"

"Sir, will you be showing us a movie? We want *Harry Potter*."

"Sir, we need a basketball coach. Can you help us?"

"Sir, can you get us pen pals? We'd like to have pen pals from America."

Behind every request, there seemed to lurk the same two words – Mr. Chris. I was really starting to dislike this guy simply because he had done such a wonderful job. It became quite apparent this was the measuring stick I would be put up against. However, I imagine he went through the same ordeal when he replaced the volunteer before him.

The learners were not the only ones getting in on the action. Teachers also approached me with their own requests.

"Mr. Wes, I just got a new computer. Could you teach me how to use it? Maybe put some fancy anti-virus on it? I bet you're good at that."

"Mr. Wes, I'm taking an advanced math class as part of an extended university course. Could you help me with my homework?"

I didn't mind helping people. But in situations like this, when you're volunteering abroad, you have to take into consideration the difference between people asking for your assistance and trying to take advantage of you. One colleague blatantly asked me to write an essay for his brother's university English class. I found it ironic he was a teacher, and was helping his brother cheat on a school essay. I flat out told him no.

In the beginning, I assumed the school's expectations of me would be high, but I just didn't think they would be so immediate. Everyone had nothing but good things to say about Mr. Chris, and I wanted them to have good things to say about me when I left, too. But I wasn't going to fill Mr Chris' shoes, simply because I wasn't planning to put them on. I wanted to make my own mark on Eengedjo.

The truth is that I wasn't too worried about letting the school down. I was, however, starting to feel the pressure about letting the kids down. Growing up, these kids didn't have luxuries like computers, smartphones, or iPods. Heck, I don't know if some of them had ever even taken a hot shower. Not that these artificial items are synonymous with happiness, but they are amenities most people choose to live with rather than without. In some ways, I couldn't help but feel bad for the kids. Yet, empathy can be a double-edged sword. I mean – let's face it – it's partly what brought me here in the first place. I wanted to teach in a struggling rural area where need was great and resources were few. But would coddling the kids really benefit their character?

When I grew up in America, I was blinded with the bright optimism that "Everybody's a winner! You can do anything if you put your mind to it." However, these learners had not been blanketed with such confidence. Many of them were accustomed to receiving low marks in school, accepted the likelihood of repeating grades, and as for attending university many felt as if it were just a pipe dream. A fair number of the learners had seen so much failure on paper that they had developed a "what's the point" kind of attitude. But shouldn't we allow kids to fail? Isn't failing one of the best ways to learn from our mistakes? These questions weighed on my conscience when I considered not only how I should treat the kids, but how I should evaluate them. Thus, my biggest concern about coddling the learners was in the classroom. It reminded me of a time during my orientation, when I had been forewarned about this very issue. I digress.

Chapter 6

The Orientation Express

Three pairs of jeans – Check!

Four pairs of shorts – Check!

Eight pairs of socks – Check!

Seven t-shirts – Check!

Five button-up shirts – Check!

Raincoat – Check!

There was no rhyme or reason to my packing method. I just started throwing clothes and accessories on top of my bed before shoving them into a large backpack. Often, this is the best way to over-pack; bring stuff just because you have it, not because you need it.

Laptop – Check!

Headlamp – Check!

Sleeping bag – Check!

Passport – Check!

Doxycycline – Check!

In order to combat malaria, an infectious disease transmitted by mosquitoes, I had loaded up on the antibiotic Doxycycline. WorldTeach puts a strong emphasis on health, and referred our group of volunteers to the Centers for Disease Control's website for information about necessary vaccinations, including measles, tetanus, polio, hepatitis A, hepatitis B, typhoid, and rabies. Fortunately, due to previous international travel, I was already chock-full of many of these vaccinations. And now that I had my malaria meds, I was ready to enter a hot zone.

After a while, my bed was littered with clothes, medicines, books, and other amenities. When I finally finished packing everything, my bags were bursting at the seams. The only item that remained on the bed was my boarding pass for the morning's flight. I folded it up and tucked it into my passport. I was now ready to become a WorldTeach volunteer.

The first time I had ever heard of the WorldTeach organization was in Costa Rica. I was working with Habitat for Humanity as a Volunteer Coordinator, and a girl who was volunteering on a housing project was previously a WorldTeach volunteer in Ecuador. She had nothing but positive things to say about the organization and her experience. I must have stored this information on a subconscious level because after teaching for a few years in South Korea, I began looking for other international teaching opportunities. One of the first places I turned to was WorldTeach. From the beginning, it felt like it was just meant to be.

WorldTeach is a non-profit organization founded in 1986 by a group of Harvard students. Its inception came about in order to address the need for educational assistance in developing countries, as well as serve a growing interest among people who wished to teach and learn as volunteers abroad. WorldTeach initially began its work in Kenya, and within five years it had grown to offer year-long programs in Namibia, Botswana, China, Thailand, Poland, Costa Rica, and Ecuador. Currently, the organization operates programs in 17 different countries worldwide, and the programs vary in length from one year to one semester to a temporary summer program. WorldTeach has grown steadily, and as of the end of 2012, over 5,000 volunteers have served internationally. The organization exists to assist people like me. I wanted a way to help others, and without WorldTeach I never would have found Namibia.

My journey officially began on December 28, 2009 when our group convened in New York City for the first time. The next morning we flew out of JFK International Airport, destination – Windhoek! The group consisted of 14 volunteers ranging in ages from 22 to 65. We were an eclectic mix of personalities, although at the time everyone tried not to wear their emotions on their sleeves. After nearly 20 hours of transit and connecting through Johannesburg, South Africa, we arrived in the capital city around noon the following day (Windhoek is six hours ahead of New York). As I stepped off the plane and into the bright daylight, all romanticized stereotypes about Africa got left behind. There was no exotic wildlife roaming around the tarmac. There was no dilapidated airport whose infrastructure was in neglect. In fact, the Hosea Kutako International Airport appeared modern and well maintained. The only preconceived notion I correctly surmised was the desert landscape, which can be credited to a Google search on Namibia.

At the airport, our group was met by Jocie, the WorldTeach Program Coordinator in Namibia. She was originally from Long Island, New York and had been living in Namibia for several years, working two years as a volunteer teacher and one year as the Program Coordinator. Jocie loved life in Namibia and had recently married a Namibian musician. She was a wealth of information, and it was nice to have someone who could show us the ropes. Soon, we had collected our baggage, piled into two different vans, and were driving to a backpacker's hostel near downtown Windhoek where we would conduct the majority of the orientation. After settling into the hostel, we were given the rest of the day to relax. The next morning we were going to hit the ground running.

Three weeks is a short amount of time to get acquainted with a new country, which meant the orientation was a whirlwind of activity and information. We talked about everything from culture and safety to shopping and cell phone services. We covered just about any issue pertinent to someone who has been transplanted in a new environment halfway across the globe. Jocie presented the material to us with a mix of documented information and personal anecdotes. We received words of wisdom which I found both revealing and peculiar. For example, girls were advised not to get too offended if a person calls them fat. Even though it's considered highly rude in Western cultures, in Namibia, commenting on a female's weight is likely meant as a compliment. Information such as this exemplified how we should deal with cultural sensitivities, especially our own.

Overall, WorldTeach administered a thorough orientation. It was a nice mix of practical instruction and fun activities. The orientation played a crucial role in preparing us for our upcoming teaching placements, but there was still much to learn. Experiences such as this are esoteric, and while remaining in Windhoek there was only so much we could take away from reading about and discussing life in Namibia. Now we just had to get out there and experience the life for ourselves. After being given the proper tools of information and understanding, I was ready to start building my future in this exotic new country.

Even though I felt more comfortable getting ready to embark on this educational journey, I was still a nervous wreck. I thought a great deal about how my relationship with the learners would unfold. Throughout the orientation we received many different pieces of advice. But strangely enough, the sagest piece of advice wasn't unearthed as part of the orientation. Of all places, I was given this advice from a gentleman at a bar.

After the first week of orientation, all the volunteers participated in a host stay over the weekend. Since there weren't enough hosts to accommodate all the volunteers individually, we separated into small groups. Three other volunteers and I were chaperoned by a gentleman named Hango, a short, thin, fun-loving guy with a perpetual smile. Hango didn't look a day over 16 years old, but we later found out he was a 24-year-old Ovambo native from the north.

Hango arrived at the hostel along with a small entourage of friends and after everyone got acquainted, we climbed into the back of an old red pickup truck and took off. We had no idea where we were going. Truthfully, I don't think Hango really knew what to do with us, so Jocie had told him to do what he normally does. He may have taken that advice to heart.

A day in the life of Hango began in the township of Katutura, perhaps the most infamous area in Windhoek. Katutura is located in the northern part of the capital and was originally formed in 1961 when black residents were forced to move from the Old Location (an area previously segregated for black residents of Windhoek). Katutura has the most condensed population within Windhoek and accounts for over half of the city's entire population. The township has some moderate economic areas, but by and large, the majority of residents live in extremely impoverished conditions. We witnessed this firsthand when Hango and his crew gave us a nickel-and-dime tour of the township.

When we first entered Katutura, we drove along pothole-ridden concrete roads with cement homes on both sides. Hango was a resident of Katutura, and he seemed to know a lot of people throughout the township because our truck slowed down on several occasions so he could greet people walking along the road. Eventually, the paved road turned into dirt and the concrete homes were replaced with shacks constructed from corrugated metal siding. The truck finally came up on a bluff overlooking the surrounding area. Corrugated metal shacks heavily dotted the hillside and the valley down below for as far as the eye could see. The truck then veered down the hill and headed straight into the heart of Katutura.

Our first stop was a neighborhood called Babylon, and it's where one can find some of the most extreme poverty within Windhoek. We drove along an unmaintained dirt road, weaving between shacks that had been randomly placed on the land as if they had fallen from the sky like raindrops. Rocks and bricks had been placed on top of the shacks, I assume to hold the roof down and keep it from falling in the midst of a storm. These shacks had no running water and very few had electricity. Those that had power did so by splicing cables from a nearby power line. There was no indoor plumbing and everyone shared communal toilets. Even though I had read about poverty in Namibia and seen pictures online, it's still tough to stomach when you see such impoverished living conditions with your own eyes.

Appropriately, the first stop that morning was at a shabeen, a little garage bar Hango said his brother owned. The truck came to a halt in front of a small concrete structure where several people were sitting out front in old lawn chairs. Hango introduced all three men as his brothers; however, the word "brother" is used loosely in Namibia and in many cases the person may not actually be a blood relative. Everyone was extremely hospitable and they offered us a Windhoek Lager, Namibia's number one beer, but it was a little too early in the morning. Instead, we embarked on a brief walking tour of Babylon.

We leisurely walked along a dirt pathway, passing one metal shack after another. While walking, we managed to get a lot of curious looks from the local residents. But everyone was very friendly and greeted us at every turn. Many of the children, who were scantily dressed and without shoes, seemed particularly excited to see us. They waved enthusiastically and giggled as we walked by.

After the walking tour, we hopped back into the truck and sped off to another shabeen where we chatted up some of the locals. After about an hour, we headed off to yet another shabeen. A pattern was beginning to emerge, and we spent the next several hours shabeen-hopping around Katutura. Eventually, we made the switch from drinking soda to Windhoek Lager. One might think that going from one shabeen to another would get old after a while, but it didn't. In

An area of Katutura

fact, it was the most exciting activity we had done since arriving in Namibia.

Many Windhoek Lagers later, we decided to get some food. Hango and his friends took us to an open-air market where we sampled *kapana*, which is Namibian street food that consists of grilled meat. Upon first glance, the market looked like a health and safety inspector's worst nightmare. Vendors had their grills set up on large stone blocks and behind them were large chunks of red meat piled on wooden tables. Behind the tables were larger slabs of meat hanging off hooks. The market not only attracted people but a number of flies as well. Fortunately, or perhaps not, the flies weren't bothering customers because they were too preoccupied buzzing around the meat.

Hmm…I wonder how many Michelin stars this place has.

As ramshackle as the market appeared, looks have never deterred me from sampling the substance of a place. I walked around to several vendors sampling the different kapana, which pretty much tasted the same. At each place the vendor would slice up bite-sized pieces of meat with a machete, unlikely to have been sterilized, and throw it on the grill. Afterwards, the meat was piled onto a paper plate. There were no forks, knives, or even napkins. Everyone ate using their hands. It was a true cultural experience.

After getting our fill of food, Hango suggested we go to a bar down the street, which happened to be next to the place where we would stay for the night. This wasn't really a "home stay" per se. The place Hango arranged for us looked more like a generic bed & breakfast. I don't know if he worked there or was friends with the owner, but it was a very confusing story. Either way, he didn't have to twist our arms to go check out the bar.

The name of the bar was Oluzizi, and when we walked in the door daylight was fading. Oluzizi wasn't like the shabeens we had been hanging around the entire day, but an actual bar. The place was decorated with neon lights and had a large open dance floor. There was even a DJ playing music on turntables.

Hango introduced us around and everyone was very receptive. Actually, we were treated like rock stars. The first question everyone would ask was, "Where are you from?" After talking about what we doing in Namibia, everyone immediately thanked us for taking an interest in their country. They even bought us drinks.

Later that evening, I went to the bar to get a beer when a gentleman next to me caught my attention. He looked to be in his late 30s and was dressed nicely in pants and a sport coat.

"So where are you from?" he asked.

"I'm from Namibia," I told him. Although I'm sure my accent was a dead giveaway.

"Really, so you're an Afrikaaner[2] then?"

---

[2] Afrikaaners are a Germanic ethnic group in Southern Africa who are descendants of Dutch, French, and German settlers.

"That's correct."

"And you speak Afrikaans?"

"Of course," I said without hesitation. He then proceeded to say something in Afrikaans. I responded with the only word I knew.

"Lekker!" This word is slang in Afrikaans, with a similar meaning to *cool* in English. It's also commonly used to describe food as being tasty. I don't know the context in which the word fell in our conversation, but the guy started laughing.

"You know what I said?" he asked.

"No idea."

"I said you Americans are pretty easy to spot." He was smiling now, and I couldn't really argue with that logic. I talked to this gentleman, whose name I don't even remember, for quite some time. He was Ovambo, and claimed to be from a village in north-central Namibia. Now he lived in Windhoek working as a maintenance manager. When I told him I would soon move to Omungwelume and teach at Eengedjo, he claimed to be familiar with the school. I shared my story as a WorldTeach volunteer and told him my friends and I were doing a home stay nearby to get better acquainted with Namibian culture.

When I finished my sentence, he told me, "Thank you."

"For what?"

"For coming here to work," he said. "What you're doing is very important. The schools up north need a great deal of help." I nodded along, our conversation suddenly taking on a more serious tone. Throughout the past week, and even before I arrived in Namibia, many people had praised my efforts in becoming a volunteer teacher. Yet, I wasn't sure how to handle such commendation. Did I really deserve it?

"I want to buy you a beer," the gentleman told me. I tried to tell him it wasn't necessary but he insisted. Eventually, I accepted his kind gesture because in some cultures it is insulting not to accept gifts.

"You know," the man continued as the bartender handed him two beers. "It's a difficult life up there."

"Yeah, I've heard there's a lot of poverty," I replied, pretending to understand his meaning.

"That's not what I'm talking about," he said. "Poverty is everywhere, like I'm sure you've seen here in Katutura. I think conditions are actually worse in the city than out in the country. But life is difficult where you're going because there are no opportunities. That's why everyone wants to come to Windhoek. It's the best place to find work."

The man was right. Besides being the capital, Windhoek is the social, economic, and cultural center of Namibia. The city is home to just about all of the country's major business enterprises. I thanked the man for the beer, and we clanked our bottles together and made a toast to Namibia. After, the man leaned in and asked, "Can I give you some advice?"

"What's that?"

"Don't pity them," he said with a solemn look. "These kids need a good education. Don't feel sorry for them just because they're poor and you think they have a rough life. Treat them just like you would treat American children. It will be best for their education."

I wasn't quite sure how to respond, so again I just nodded my head. I understood what he was getting at, even though I had never actually taught American children. I shouldn't allow my empathy to treat these kids differently. I should encourage them, not coddle them. I should motivate them, not spoil them. I was about to be exposed to a world much different than my own, and I had to keep in mind that I was here to teach these kids, not just be their friend.

This random piece of advice struck a chord with me throughout the year, as I frequently reminded myself of this conversation. Perhaps it should have been the other way around, and I should have bought him the beer.

Chapter 7
This Isn't Kansas Anymore!

Shortly after I arrived at Eengedjo, I was playing basketball one afternoon with some of the older boys. Running around in the hot Namibian sun, I quickly broke out into a full sweat and soon looked like I had just participated in a wet t-shirt contest. The powdery dirt from the school grounds got kicked up in the air and stuck to my skin. When we finished playing, I was in desperate need of a shower. I was as dirty as the donkeys that rolled around on the dusty ground just outside my house. After the game, I went back home, put the basketball away, and headed straight for the shower. I turned the nozzle and the showerhead began spitting out short bursts of air.

Hmm...this is not good.

The pipes continued to wheeze as if they had whooping cough, until the air pressure equalized and then there was complete silence. I tried not to think about what would happen if my water was out for the rest of the day. I decided to leave the tap open so that when the water returned, I would hear it running. In the meantime, I watched some TV programs which I had downloaded on my computer.

After about an hour, I heard the sound of splashing water. It was music to my ears, but when I assessed the situation it wasn't as I had dreamt it would be. Water spilled slowly out from the showerhead and smacked the tile floor, which unpleasantly reminded me of someone peeing. But beggars can't be choosers. I climbed into the shower and immediately noticed the next peculiarity of my situation. Since there was hardly any water pressure, the stream fell only several inches from the wall. In a series of ballet-like motions, I positioned each sector of my body under the water and washed the dirt away. The feeling of cold water on my face was a relief, and I grabbed a bottle of shampoo to lather up my hair. But just as I was about to stick my head under the water and wash out the suds, the bladder emptied. Slowly, the water came to a trickle, then there were just a few drops, and finally the showerhead began wheezing again.

Hmm…this is not good.

I pondered my dilemma for a moment and suddenly had an idea. In the kitchen there were a bunch of two-liter plastic Coke bottles full of water. Up until then, I was keeping these bottles as emergency drinking water. Now they had become emergency shower water. I quickly went to the kitchen to grab a bottle. Then I returned to the shower and dumped the water on my head to wash my hair. Afterwards, I had an epiphany. I was going to have to shave my head.

The next day, I placed several plastic Coke bottles full of water in my bathroom. Never in my life had it been necessary to plan my day in accordance to the availability of water. Ultimately, I was forced to become more conscious of my water consumption since I would typically have to use my bottled-water supply a few times a week. Then when I had to fill my toilet tank so I could flush it, I really began to understand just how much water we consume in the developed world and how easily we take it for granted.

It didn't take long before a pattern began to unfold. Although the times were not exact, just about every day in the afternoon/early evening I would lose running water for a few hours. The school's water came from a well, and there was a small water tower behind the dining hall where water was drawn. At times when water use on the school grounds was high, such as in the morning and late afternoon, the tower would drain quickly and all the taps would run dry. Once this happened, I would just have to wait. This wasn't the ideal living situation, but then again, everything is relative. Compared to some other volunteer placements, I was in Shangri-La. I was fortunate to even have running water since other volunteers had to fetch their water from a nearby source and carry it back home. It's ironic how the world's most abundant resource can seemingly be so scarce. But such was the case in most areas of rural Namibia.

Electricity was another fickle amenity. Even though electricity was a bit more consistent than my water supply, it had no reliable schedule. Blackouts were frequent, although most of the time they would last no more than ten minutes. But when the lights went out for good, all was quiet and there was nothing to do but go to sleep. Still, compared to other volunteer situations I was fortunate to have somewhat consistent power.

While working in Namibia, I would no longer get pampered with certain amenities, some of which I had forgotten how to live without. I would have to adjust my lifestyle and adapt because these annoyances had become facts of life. Replenishing water bottles when running water was available became a weekly chore. I also had to make sure plenty of candles were on hand for when the power went out. It's interesting how quickly a person can adapt to uncomfortable situations, especially when you know there is nothing you can do about it. For better or for worse, these modern inconveniences were now part of my normal life in Omungwelume.

School was another acclimation process altogether. Class sizes in Namibia were much larger than what I was accustomed to with around 40 learners in most classes. There were also fewer resources at my disposal since basic school supplies such as chalk, erasers, and the ability to make copies were not always available. Yet, one of the greatest challenges was getting accustomed to the classroom culture. Some cultural traits were hard to accept, while others were hard to maintain.

Donkeys resting just outside my home

One of the first behaviors I noticed when I began teaching was the snapping of fingers. If learners knew the answer, they would snap their fingers at me. If they had a question, they would snap their fingers at me. If they wanted to get my attention for any reason at all, they would snap their fingers at me.

Wow, that's really annoying.

Not all of the kids would snap, as some would quietly raise their hand. But for the most part, every time I asked a question, there would be an outbreak of snapping sounds. Even though we had been informed about this classroom custom in orientation, to me snapping sounded rude and disrespectful. But I knew it wasn't intended to be malicious. In fact, it was just the opposite. The kids who were snapping were the ones who were engaged in the lesson. And the more they were engaged, the more they would snap. Snapping was an ingrained part of their education, and ultimately it was easier for me to adapt than for them to break the habit. Besides, if you can't beat'em, join'em! In order to accept this classroom mannerism, I started snapping in class. When I would call on someone for the answer, I would snap my fingers and point in their direction. That learner would rise from their chair – if they weren't already standing due to a lack of chairs – and answer the question, which illustrated another part of classroom culture.

When answering questions in class, learners would habitually stand to give their answer as though they were getting ready to give a speech. In Ovambo culture, when a person addresses a group, the speaker is expected to stand. At first, I remember disliking this classroom norm. Since the learners' physical movements were typically slow and methodical, they often took their time when standing. Sometimes they would stand just to answer a *yes or no* question. Initially, I thought this was an incredible waste of time because it slowed down the class. But as I acclimated to this norm, I began to see some of the benefits. When the learners stood to answer questions, this shifted the attention from me to the class, and many of them were inclined to pay attention to what their peers had to say. Also, the learners enjoyed having the spotlight, so answering questions became motivation to stay involved in the lesson. Over time, I accepted this custom and no longer gave it much thought.

Another standing mannerism of Namibian school culture takes place when teachers enter the classroom. Typically, the entire class would stand, and kids are taught this school tradition from a very young age. The reason for this is that it projects a structured form of discipline and shows respect for the teacher. The very first week, many of the classes stood when I entered. However, that practice quickly died out, and eventually only the younger grades would stand for me. At first, I was slightly disheartened the learners wouldn't stand. I had a fleeting delusion that by the end of the year I would earn their respect, and all the learners would be on top of their desks proclaiming, "Oh captain, my captain." It's probably good that they didn't because the desks were so feeble they would all just topple over.   But my disappointment waned when I noticed Eengedjo learners didn't stand for all the Namibian teachers either. Perhaps the custom is changing, since in many Western countries this practice is considered old-fashioned. Later, I would come to realize that this was my first of many lessons on how customs and traditions are changing with each generation.

Chapter 8

The Hitchhiker's Guide to Omungwelume

Hike (*noun*)
An informal method of transportation in Namibia utilized by people without cars in order to get from one area to the next. Cars, typically filled well beyond capacity, travel to their destination while evading potholes, donkeys, livestock, and people (normal Namibian road obstacles). The fare of a hike is an established price determined by the distance traveled.

As I walked out onto the tar road – "paved road" in American English – which ran through the heart of little Omungwelume, I looked to see if there were any cars around. The shoulderless road was quiet, so I ambled towards a mini-mart at the far end of the village where drivers would give people a lift to town. Every so often, I turned back to see if a vehicle was coming my way. Within a minute, I spotted a car off on the horizon barreling down the road. I flailed my right arm and pointed in the direction I wanted to go. Destination – Oshakati!

About once a week, I made a trip into Oshakati to run errands. With a population of 33,618 people, Oshakati is considered the largest town in north-central Namibia. It's also thought of as the unofficial capital of Ovamboland. But most importantly, being roughly 30 km away, it was the closest place where I could find any semblance of development.

The car approached me at full speed, and perhaps the driver didn't see me until the last minute. The small sedan came to a screeching halt, without a doubt jerking forward the other passengers inside. It stopped about 25 meters in front of me, and I could see the people inside shuffling around to make room. If I were anywhere else, I probably would have hurried to the car. However, while living in Omungwelume I was doing my best to gravitate towards the local pace of life. I leisurely made my way to the idling vehicle and opened the side door.

I climbed in and said hello to my fellow passengers, and everyone greeted me in return. Counting me, there were eight people in this little sedan. It wasn't as uncomfortable as it may sound since several of the passengers were less than three feet tall. A husband and wife (I presume) sat in the back with me and had their two kids on their laps. Another man was in the front passenger's seat with a small child who I didn't even notice until we reached Oshakati.

The driver pulled the car back onto the tar road, and we were off. At least, I thought we were. A few seconds after picking me up, the driver pulled back off the road and parked in front of the mini-mart I had originally been walking towards. In terms of a "hike," this was a vintage Namibian layover. Frequently, drivers would pull over, make random stops, or slow down to converse with other people on the road. This could turn the shortest of distances into the most epic of journeys. Driving nonstop from Omungwelume to Oshakati would take less than 20 minutes. However, my personal record for the longest hike between these two places – taking into account waiting for the car to fill up with passengers, getting gas, dropping people off, picking more people up, stopping by the driver's grandmother's house, and pulling over to fix the radio – was 1 hour and 47 minutes.

As it turned out, our driver was the one who needed something at the mini-mart. He exited the car, and the rest of us waited patiently. About a minute later, the man reemerged carrying a 40-

ounce bottle of Black Label beer. He hopped back behind the wheel, and we sped off down the road.

Drinking and driving is a serious concern in Namibia. Most countries throughout the world have their fair share of problems with this issue, and Namibia is no exception. In orientation, we were forewarned that we would likely be confronted with the decision of whether or not to get in the car with a person who had been drinking. But out in the rural countryside, if a person does not own a car, getting a hike is practically a must. The only other option is to walk. Now, I would love to say this was the only instance in which I had ridden with someone who was either under the influence or trying to achieve that state of mind, but that's just not reality. As we drove down the road, my only hope was that this guy was breaking into his first beer of the day.

With one quick motion, the driver popped off the bottle cap with his tooth. This is common practice in Namibia, and it may have even been a rite of passage for most Namibian males. Everyone I met knew how to do it. I had tested the durability of my own teeth on several occasions with varying success, but then I remembered how expensive dental work is back in America.

As the driver took a hefty swig from his Black Label, I checked my surroundings for a seatbelt. I knew it was a long shot since most of the cars used for hikes are old and run-down. I would be lucky if I had a functioning door handle, let alone a seatbelt. But alas, I discovered a safety belt. The gods must have been smiling on me that day, but perhaps they were shaking their heads at the same time because, much to my dismay, there was nowhere to buckle it.

Our captain passed the bottle of beer to the man sitting next to me in the back seat. This didn't come as a surprise since, culturally, it's common courtesy to share. The man took a couple of sips and then held it out for me to indulge.

What an incredibly nice gesture. Who knew I would have found a hike serving free drinks?

The tar road leading out of Omungwelume and towards Oshakati

I politely declined, and so did the other gentleman sitting in the passenger's seat. The bottle quickly found its way back into the hands of the driver, and I started to second-guess my sound judgment. Perhaps the safest action would have been for me to slam the entire beer. But the beer's alcohol content provided me with some level of comfort because the vast majority of brands contain only 4% alcohol. Fortunately, our passage to town was without incident, and since everyone in the car was on their way to Oshakati, there were no further delays.

When we arrived in Oshakati, the driver let me out near the open street market, the nucleus of the town's commercial area. I paid the man $13 Namibian, which is a little less than $2 U.S., and exited the vehicle. (The exchange rate from Namibian dollars to U.S. dollars was 7:1.) The street market in Oshakati was full of stalls that sold a variety of clothes, accessories, and local snack food. As I walked through the market, I passed old ladies with large burlap sacks full of mopani worms. This local snack is extremely popular in northern Namibia and is supposedly a great source of protein. In truth, mopani worms are actually disemboweled caterpillars that have been dried and boiled in saltwater before being preserved in ashes. Sound delicious? They are called mopani because they feed off of the indigenous mopani tree. I tried mopani worms on several occasions, and I don't know how else to describe the flavor except that they tasted like earth.

On the other side of the street market was the Etango Centre, one of the principal shopping areas in Oshakati. Here I began my weekly shopping routine. After hitting up the bank to take out money, I went next door to grab a bite to eat at KFC. As far as dining in Oshakati is concerned, the list of restaurants begins and ends with KFC, which is by far the most popular food chain throughout the country. After eating some greasy fried chicken, I walked across the street to a camera store to print out pictures. On any given week, I would have about 50 pictures to print out. Since the learners loved pictures, I started using them as a method of rewards in the classroom, which was a great motivator. Finally, my last stop was at a grocery store called Pick n Pay. My ritual shopping list included a loaf of bread, two packets of sandwich meat, one pack of processed cheese, three Lipton pasta dishes, two bags of Lays Thai Sweet Chili[3] crisps (potato chips), one two-liter bottle of Coca-Cola, and two bottles of a wine called Tall Horse, which is an inexpensive South African wine I bought simply because I liked the giraffe on its label. Once my shopping needs were met, I shoved everything into my backpack and then found a taxi to take me to the Omungwelume hike point.

---

[3] The Thai Sweet Chili potato chips are hands down the best potato chips I've ever had. It's a mystery why they don't sell these chips in America. My letters to Lays have proved unsuccessful.

In Oshakati, there are designated hike points where cars wait to take people to specific areas. Omungwelume's hike point was located at the Shell gas station on the west side of town. Every time I got a hike back home, it was the same old story. As soon as I arrived at the Shell station, absolute chaos would ensue. At the hike point I was always greeted by a host of individuals, which included not only drivers jockeying for passengers but other random people who were helping these drivers fill their cars. It's the latter who were more demanding and forceful. Usually, they were young boys who had likely dropped out of school and had few options to earn money. The drivers would pay them a small commission if they could convince people to ride in their vehicle. The tricky part about this operation was the lack of a queue. It was a free-for-all with every man, woman, and child for themselves.

After a while, I developed a game plan for when I arrived at the hike point. It pretty much entailed pushing everyone out of the way and trying to find a car that already had passengers, which meant it would leave sooner. On one of my first trips to Oshakati, I let a guy usher me to an empty vehicle and I had to wait a half hour before the car filled up. On this day, however, I had made a mistake. My backpack was in the trunk of the taxi. I wasn't worried about it getting stolen, but people had to be careful with their belongings because the guys who worked at the hike point would use whatever leverage possible to coerce people to their vehicle. I once saw a guy inconspicuously walk off with a small child and put the kid in his car while the mother helplessly tried to secure her grocery bags. And it worked! She eventually saw her child sitting in the back seat and walked over to put her stuff inside the vehicle.

Because I was in no mood to get bombarded by people, I told the taxi driver to drop me off a little ways beyond the hike point. But it was too late. I had been spotted. By now, most of the people at the hike point knew who I was, which came as no surprise since I was the only white person living in Omungwelume. As we drove by, four individuals began running alongside the taxi. "Eengedjo! Eengedjo! Eengedjo!" they kept yelling. Immediately after the taxi stopped, everyone was pushing and shoving each other to open the door for me. I quickly handed the driver his money so I could run to the trunk and dive-bomb on top of my backpack. However, the driver popped the trunk before I could get out of the car. The alarms bells in my head went off.

NOOOO!

As soon as my "helpers" heard the trunk pop, they let me go and quickly ran to examine the contents inside. They knew that carrying my belongings was the most effective way to get my business. It didn't take long before two guys started wrestling for control of my backpack. Another man came over and tried to help his friend by pealing one of the assailants off my pack. It was a mid-afternoon royal rumble, and they were all yelling at one another in Oshikwanyama. I decided to get in on the action. I pushed one guy aside and grabbed one of the shoulder straps, sliding my arm through it. I thought this would clearly give me possession of the pack. However, another guy had slid his arm through the other shoulder strap.

"What are you doing?" I demanded.

"Sir, I'm helping you. Follow me! Follow me!" He didn't seem convinced to release his hold.

"Let go of the pack," I said calmly.

At this point, I found some of our confrontations rather amusing. He just wanted to help me so he could get his kickback of a few Namibian dollars. On occasion, I would let people assist me to a car. But when there was a crowd of people, I would always decline their assistance. The Good Samaritan eventually released his grip, and I pulled the pack onto my shoulders. There were six people crowded around me saying, "Sir, you're going to Eengedjo. Come with me! Come with me now!"

I pushed my way through the crowd in order to get a look at the vehicles. There were four cars in the area, and only one had passengers in it. Unfortunately, it looked full. However, the word *full* doesn't exist in hike terminology. As I examined the car, a gentleman came over and put his arm around me. "My friend, you come with us," he said and pointed at the full vehicle. "We go, now now now." This is a nuance of Namibian English. If a person says "now," they really mean *later*. If they say "now now," it means *soon*. And when they say, "now now now," it actually means *now*.

"You sure I can fit?" I asked the man, who happened to be the driver.

"My friend, we have plenty of room."

There was a young, heavyset female in the passenger's seat, and in the back were crammed two old ladies, a young man, and two children. Before even making sure it was physically possible for me to get in the car, the driver took my backpack and wedged it into the trunk, which was also full with a spare tire and several bags of rice. It took a few tries to get the trunk to close, but once it did, it was official. I was riding with them. The driver told the girl sitting in the front to move over, and I climbed in. The two of us uncomfortably shared the seat, but this was a typical seating arrangement for a hike. Actually, I was quite fortunate to have a window seat.

Typically, the rides back to Omungwelume would take a little longer than the rides to Oshakati. We would make stops along the road in completely remote areas. People would climb out of the car, gather their belongings, and disappear off into the bush. I could only assume their home or village was located somewhere back there. When we arrived in Omungwelume, I was let out on the main road and had to walk back to the school. If I was lucky, drivers would sometimes drop me at the front gates of Eengedjo, which would earn them a couple of extra Namibian dollars. For the entire year, this was my weekly routine, and these trips into town would usually take several hours.

When I first heard about the public transport system, I thought it might be a cumbersome part of rural living. However, it just took some time to get used to it. To be honest, the first time I was exposed to such aggressive behavior at a hike point, it was a little intimidating. I thought everyone was being overly forceful because I was a foreigner. But other Namibians were treated the same way. When it came to getting a hike, it truly was survival of the fittest.

Chapter 9
Making the Grade, or Not

Two weeks after I began teaching at Eengedjo, I was getting ready to pass back my English class's first quiz. The top paper in the stack of quizzes was heavily marked in red pen. In the corner I had written 40%. Trying to convey my sense of disapproval, I handed it to the boy with a slight glower. He looked at the paper without reacting. To him, it was just a number. The rest of the quizzes ranged from 20% to 75%. Most of the learners displayed little concern for their low marks. On the contrary, some were enthusiastic. The girl who received a 75% proceeded to brag to her neighbors. Another boy, who scored 65%, earnestly said to me, "Thank you sir. It was not too difficult."

Not too difficult! You barely got over half of them right.

I didn't verbally express my frustration to the boy, and the sincerity of his comment caught me off guard. Overall, the class average came out to around 50%. My other English class didn't fare much better and averaged about 55%. If anything, these marks were disconcerting, and I was a bit distraught by the learners' performance. Furthermore, nobody challenged me on any of the questions they got wrong. Normally I would expect some dispute over grades, especially those this low. However, everyone seemed to accept their mark and was ready to move on with their lives. So what was I missing? These grades were unacceptable, right?

Typically, I'm pretty adaptable when it comes to cultural quirks, social expectations, and religious differences. I would rather learn something than challenge someone, would rather try something new before attempting to convert someone to my way of thinking. After spending a fair amount of time abroad, I've been able to accept a myriad of ways in which people go about their lives. But professionally speaking, this was a bit different. For some reason, I had a tough time accepting Namibia's educational expectations. I never really considered the country might have a completely different grading scale worlds apart from my own. I ignorantly assumed the evaluation of learners would be on par with the grading standards I grew up with. In my opinion, a 65% was no reason to thank the teacher. Or was it?

When traveling abroad, it's important to keep an open mind. Still, people have a natural tendency to compare another country's customs to their own. And since a person usually considers their own views as the standard of correctness, any differences can invariably lead to shock, otherwise known as culture shock. In coming to Namibia, my greatest shock was when I first saw the country's grading schematic.

When it came to performance expectations, I wasn't on the same page as the MOE. Initially, I felt that I should hold the learners to a higher standard and expect them to perform accordingly. It never occurred to me that perhaps some were performing to a high standard and I just wasn't able to acknowledge it. As for grading, I had a tough time accepting the "everything is relative" train of thought. To me, 50% was failing, not satisfactory. And I never imagined 30% would ever be a passing grade.

This bar is so low it's not even getting off the ground.

Why, then, were so many Eengedjo learners receiving extremely low marks? If the bar was so low, you would think learners wouldn't "fail" to jump over it.

Grades	Mark Range	Grade Descriptions
A	80%+	Achieved Basic Competencies exceptionally well.
B	70 – 79%	Achieved Basic Competencies very well.
C	60 – 69%	Achieved Basic Competencies well.
D	50 – 59%	Achieved Basic Competencies satisfactory.
E	40 – 49%	Achieved a sufficient number of Basic Competencies.
F	30 – 39%	Achieved the Basic Competencies needed to be considered competent.
G	20 – 29%	Achieved the minimum number of Basic Competencies worthy of a grade.
U	0 – 19%	Did not achieve the minimum level of competencies.

Grading scale taken from a form circulated by the MOE in 2010 and outlines promotional requirements for secondary education

Prior to coming to Namibia, I was familiar with the grading schematic in America, where I grew up, and South Korea, where I previously taught. Though America and Korea have very different educational systems, their numerical evaluations are similar. I was unfamiliar with letter grades such as *U*. One would think a letter that far back in the alphabet would be demoralizing. (Logically, *U* stands for *ungraded*.) Yet, this grading scale is not solely Namibia's but part of the International General Certificate of Secondary Education (IGCSE).

If learners successfully complete their secondary education, they are presented with a Namibia Senior Secondary Educational Certificate, which is equivalent to the IGCSE. The IGCSE is an internationally-recognized qualification for school learners and was developed by the University of Cambridge International Examinations in 1988. Cambridge International Examinations is widely influential across educational institutions, and currently learners in over 150 different countries are taking the organization's exams.

Using the Cambridge system, the learners of secondary education are evaluated on a number scale and given a letter grade. In turn, each letter grade corresponds to a number of points. The IGCSE is graded on an 8-point scale, with letter grades ranging from *A** to *G* (*A** is equivalent to what other countries may refer to as an *A*+, and is given to marks 90 – 100%). Therefore, an *A** receives 8 points, an *A* receives 7 points, a *B* receives 6 points, and so on down to a *U*, which receives 0 points. The points learners accumulate ultimately determine whether or not they will be promoted to the next grade level. However, not all classes count.

Learners in Namibia take a variety of subjects, which are deemed either promotional or non-promotional. Marks are given for promotional subjects only, and non-promotional subjects have no bearing on a learner's academic record. For example, my computer class was a non-promotional subject, so I didn't have to evaluate the learners. Therefore, learners, as well as teachers, understandably place more importance on promotional subjects, especially English.

Within secondary education, promotional requirements vary by grade. As of 2010, according to the requirements set by the MOE, in order for learners in grades 8 and 9 to be promoted, they have to receive E grades or better in six out of nine promotional subjects, including English and Math, and F grades or better in the remaining three subjects. This sets the minimum point total for promotion at 24 points. In grade 10, learners also receive reports based on the aforementioned grading scale. However, grade 10 learners are primarily evaluated at the end of the year when they take their national assessment exam, which is a major hurdle during secondary education. Arguably, one could infer that once learners reach grade 10, they no longer get pushed along within the system.

The first few years after independence, the education system was stricken with high learner repetition rates. Then in 1994, in order to combat these high rates, the MOE implemented a policy which stated learners were allowed to repeat a grade only once in each school phase. Between grades 1 – 9, this limited the number of repetitions to three: once in lower primary, once in upper primary, and once in junior secondary. For example, if a learner failed grade 8, the first year of junior secondary, they would repeat it the next year. If the learner failed again, they would automatically be moved to grade 9 having already failed once during that school phase. Also, according to policy, learners in grade 10 can repeat only if they are under 17 years of age or if there are exceptional reasons, such as illness. Basically, in order to meet this age requirement alone, learners could not have failed any previous year of their education. This has ultimately created a large strain on the entire system.

During the 2007 school year, promotion rates for grades 7, 8, and 9 were 77.1%, 65.3%, and 71.4%, respectively. In grade 10, there was a sharp decline in the promotion rate, which dropped to a shocking 53%. So what happens to these learners who are not promoted? Unfortunately, many end up dropping out of school. In that same year, 2007, the respective drop-out rates in grades 7, 8, and 9 were 6.6%, 9.5%, and 7.7%. The grade 10 drop-out rate shot up to 24.8%, which meant about one-fourth of all grade 10 learners in Namibia dropped out of school at the end of 2007.

In senior secondary – grades 11 and 12 – learners follow a different schematic and policy. Learners are evaluated in six different promotional subjects, and passing requirements are a bit obscure. In order to receive a *Pass* on their reports, they must have at least a D in English and a total of 25 points in five subjects, including English. Therefore, if learners fail English, it doesn't matter what they do in any of the other subjects. Their final report would say *Fail*.

Once a learner is promoted to senior secondary school, grades 11 and 12 are essentially one two-year course. Both years are primarily devoted to preparing learners for the national exam. Therefore, it's essentially impossible to fail grade 11. The following is taken from a directorate circulated by the MOE in 2010:

> *Learners whose attendance, application to school work during the year, and Grade 11 examination results are satisfactory shall progress to the second year of the Senior Secondary program in Grade 12.*

Since the MOE provides a nebulous clarification as to the promotional procedures for grade 11 learners, schools blindly promote learners to grade 12, and the formal grading scale doesn't come into play. In 2007, the promotion rate of grade 11 learners was an astounding 95%, and the drop-out rate was an extremely low 3%. After learning this policy, it made me wonder why I was giving marks to my grade 11 English classes in the first place. Upon consulting the head of the language department, I was urged to try and convince the learners these marks actually counted. But everyone knew grade 11 was virtually a practice year for grade 12. Eventually, I stopped recording the marks, but I continued to mark assignments only to show learners their progress.

It's important to note that the school year in Namibia is divided into three terms, and towards the end of each term, the learners complete examinations in all their promotional subjects to give them a sense of their progress. Unfortunately, progress was rather dismal. Each term, I was given the responsibility of creating progress reports for the learners. Because I was the school's de-facto IT guy, the principal asked me to input the grades onto a spreadsheet so the reports could be generated. This meant I was given access to every learner's grade at Eengedjo. And the results were like a punch in the gut.

The very last day of each term, before the learners left to go on holiday, they received their progress reports. In the first two terms, over 85% of the learners left school with a report that read *Fail*. Many learners didn't pass English, which automatically prompted this failure. Others didn't meet the minimum requirements for the other subjects. When I asked the principal if this percentage of failure was normal, he said it was. He also asserted that it should motivate them to work harder. This may be the case for some, yet I think many learners have seen so much failure that it has contributed to an unprecedented level of apathy. Thus, how can teachers motivate their learners to work hard when poor grades have become the established norm? It even becomes more difficult with grade 11 learners who pretty much know their promotion to grade 12 is all but assured.

So what was the typical day like for an Eengedjo learner? Well, Eengedjo Secondary School is a hostel school. This means learners live on the school grounds and remain there throughout the term, visiting family and friends only on designated "home weekends." Since households in rural areas are spread far out across the countryside with poor access to roads, hostel schools were established to address this dilemma. Yet there are still not enough schools given the number of learners. Therefore, many schools are overcrowded, and Eengedjo is no different. The year I was there, the school's hostel was filled slightly beyond capacity with over four hundred learners calling it home, just over half of the entire student body. Living space was tight as learners slept in dorm rooms that could accommodate anywhere from 12 to 16 people per room. Hostel meals were about as luxurious as the living situation, and at times the kids' entire dinner consisted of only bread. Nevertheless, most of the learners wanted to stay in the hostel as opposed to living outside the school gates.

Due to hostel limitations, some kids were not admitted and were forced to find other accommodations in or around Omungwelume. Some of the older learners chose to live outside and rented small houses with their peers, sharing the space with up to 10 other learners. Other kids lived at home with their families and walked to and from school. Some learners lived as far as five kilometers away, which may not seem very far, but given the leisurely pace of Namibians, it would take them well over an hour to walk. Thus, Eengedjo was comprised of two types of learners, hostel learners and day learners.

During the school day, learners would have classes from 7 a.m. until 12:45 p.m., and afterwards everyone would get a little over an hour for lunch. Then in the afternoon, from 2 to 4 p.m. (except Friday's), the learners returned to the classrooms for afternoon study. Each class would remain in a designated room to either study or do homework. After the study session finished, the school day was officially over. The teachers were free to leave, and most of the day learners would start heading home.

Those who lived in the hostel would find different ways to occupy their time until dinner. Many kids played sports, and although the athletic fields weren't in the best condition, Eengedjo was fortunate enough to have a soccer field, basketball court, and netball court.[4] After I managed to get most of the school computers working, a lot of kids played in the computer room. Every afternoon they would cram three to a chair in front of a screen. Even with these recreational outlets, there were still many kids who seemed content just sitting around, watching the world spin and not doing anything. This ultimately embellished my stereotypical view of rural life. If I had to sum up my experience with some photographs, one picture would definitely be of a group of kids sitting under a tree.

---

[4] Netball is a very popular sport among females in Namibia.

At around 6 p.m., all activities came to a halt and everyone made their way to the dining hall for dinner. After eating, the hostel learners returned to their classrooms for evening study from 7 to 9 p.m. To the untrained eye, it seemed as though there was a great deal of time throughout the day allocated to study. But what I noticed, upon further inspection, was that many learners were not using this time to study or do homework. They were just sitting there!

Do these kids not have any homework?

Homework was something I would bombard the learners with. My English and math classes frequently mentioned to me that I gave too much homework. But there's a difference between giving homework and enforcing homework, which was one of the first challenges I faced at Eengedjo. Since learners in my grade 11 English classes knew they would get pushed on to grade 12 no matter what, there was really no academic consequence for not doing homework. They could fail, of course, but that really didn't mean much. Knowing this, I really admired those learners who completed their homework because it showed just how much they valued their education. As for the other learners, I didn't want to give them a free pass and I wasn't planning to take it easy on them.

In order to motivate learners, I used generosity as a weapon. Often the learners wanted something from me. They wanted me to take their photograph. They wanted me to show them a movie. They wanted to use the computer room. I was running a racket of extra-curricular activities. And, if anything, I wanted to teach them that nothing in life is free. In exchange for doing favors for the learners, all I asked for in return was for them to do their homework and pay attention in class. Thus, everything became *quid pro quo*.

So what about the homework in other classes? Some learners gave me the impression homework was rather optional. There were neither rewards nor consequences. Granted, most other teachers were not able to apply my methods since I had a technological leg up on them. But educators really need to think outside the box and motivate learners by other means than just stamping *FAIL* on progress reports.

Without accountability for hard work and success, how can anyone expect the educational bar to get raised accordingly? By having learners stay on task and complete the work expected of them, the country could hold everyone to a higher standard. But there are still many questions, apart from learner apathy and teacher indifference, that need to be addressed. For starters, are teachers effectively teaching the material? The bottom line is the amount of time allocated for "study" is certainly not reflected in the learners' final grades.

A class of grade 11 learners during afternoon study

Overall, the teaching methodology I witnessed in Namibia was largely ineffective. But to be fair, teachers in rural areas are given few resources, and many classes don't have the luxury of textbooks. Often, teachers are the only ones with a textbook and learners are forced to copy the material into their notebooks. The problem, however, is copying does not entail understanding. In addition, the teacher's explanation may not always match the substance of the material written in the textbooks. The end result is that many of the learners are not learning.

In Namibia, lesson summaries reign supreme. Teachers write summaries up on the board and learners reproduce the material in their notebooks. This greatly slows the learning process, as copying means less time for classroom discussion. In some cases, writing the summary is the entire lesson. So why proceed in such a way? Well, for starters, the focus remains on keeping up with curriculum requirements. Thus, quantity of material trumps its understanding and application. When I first started teaching at Eengedjo, I was also guilty of this. My math class was moving way too fast for some learners, and I had to hit the brakes. The entire course was mapped out on an instruction plan that detailed the material I needed to cover. But math is a series of connecting the dots. Learning one application is necessary to understand future material. If I tried to keep up with the instruction plan and the learners didn't understand, I would leave many of them behind. Therefore, I slowed down significantly and tried to move as fast as the slowest learner. In the end, the kids had a better understanding of the material, but we had fallen behind. Thus, in order to catch up, I held additional lessons in afternoon and evening study.

The English language was another problem when it came to comprehension, and this extended across every single subject being taught. Sometimes, I would walk into a classroom and material from the previous lesson was still up on the board. Since I taught English, I was pretty well in tune with the learners' language capabilities. I might find a science lesson on the board with words like *symbiotic* and *photosynthesis*. Very few learners could tell me the meaning of these words without using a dictionary. I would then spend a brief moment going over their science lesson before starting my own. Whether the teacher didn't have time to dissect the material or perhaps lacked the know-how, some of the learners didn't understand what they were copying.

Teacher training has been identified as a priority by the MOE. According to a 2011 article in *The Namibian*, the country's leading newspaper, there are few teachers who have specialized training and are capable of effectively administering lessons at different grade levels. A shortage of teachers has also been identified in subjects like mathematics, accounting, languages, and computer skills. Inevitably, these shortages tend to hit rural areas the hardest where teaching capacities may be given to people with minimal qualifications or even remain unfulfilled.

Even with all of its imperfections, Eengedjo was still a role model for other schools. From what I observed, many of the teachers tried hard and showed a genuine passion for the learners' success. However, there were times when I saw teachers sitting in a chair playing on their phone while one of the learners wrote the summary up on the board. Still, in my opinion, Eengedjo functioned better than other rural contemporaries for a couple of reasons. Overall, the school had better teachers and more resources. And that is a scary thought.

When it comes to providing an education, teachers certainly need to be held accountable for getting learners to perform to a higher standard. Unfortunately, I can't profess to practice what I preach. As time went on, instead of maintaining a higher grading standard, I acclimated to the established scale. Suddenly, a 60% started looking pretty good. It wasn't long before I was giving out high fives and congratulations to grades that beforehand I would have considered pitiful. It made me wonder whether I was helping to encourage improvement or tolerating mediocrity. And that's perhaps the underlying question when it comes to education. Are things really getting better?

Before independence, Namibia was comprised of several ethnic education systems, and these systems were a reflection of the policies under South Africa's apartheid. Schools were divided along racial lines, and the allocation of resources was greatly uneven. Once Namibia gained independence in 1990, reforms in education were a high priority. The different ethnic education systems were going to be brought together under one umbrella. The new government set out to restructure the system, keeping in mind five educational goals: access, equity, quality, democracy, and efficiency.

Shortly after independence, significant changes in the education system were underway. The National Institution for Education and Development (NIED) was the branch of government entrusted to make sound policies and develop a curriculum. NIED integrated a national language policy with English as the official language. The new language policy was slowly phased in, and within a few years, it became required that all school subjects from grade four and up be taught in English. In order to promote higher education, in 1992 the University of Namibia (UNAM) was established. At the time, one of UNAM's primary focuses involved teacher-training so the country could develop the skills of those who continue educating its youth. Then, to offer assistance to learners who dropped out of school, the Namibian College of Open Learning (NAMCOL) was established in 1994. Learners can take NAMCOL courses to raise their grades in subjects they previously failed, such as English, and the college also offers a national exam in order for learners to receive a diploma. Assisting in Namibia's educational reforms was Cambridge International Examinations, who partnered alongside the country's

MOE and became the exam board behind Namibia's national assessment exams.

Comparing the Namibia of today with the Namibia just after independence, some of the results look promising. More children are attending schools, the number of teachers has increased by almost 30%, and over 3,000 new classrooms have been built. In 2010, the bar of educational expectations was raised to include mathematics, along with English, as a subject that learners in secondary school had to receive an *E* grade or better – an *F* would no longer be sufficient – in order to be promoted. But even with such improvements, the topic of education remains highly contentious, as some people feel there is a difference between saying something has "***Improved***," and saying it is "***Improving***."

Since 2000, statistics among learner promotion, repetition, and drop-out rates have remained relatively stagnant. In some cases, they have moved in the wrong direction. Still, many contend the significant decline in repetition rates is due to policy changes rather than better education. As for NAMCOL, the institution has provided learners who have dropped out of school another chance at continuing their education. However, there are fees associated with NAMCOL, and learners must pay a fixed amount per subject as well as a registration fee. This puts a greater financial burden on learners and their families, especially in rural areas, who may not have the disposable income. Others have criticized the Cambridge system of education that the country has embraced. Critics claim national assessments are unfair and without merit, and therefore favor holding regional examinations instead. Then there are some disturbing statistics. It is estimated that only 12% of learners throughout Namibia continue with any sort of tertiary education due to limited space at universities and vocational schools. All these factors point to one inevitable fact. The ones who are really suffering from Namibia's educational shortcomings are the children.

The trouble with just about any argument nowadays is that people can easily piece together certain facts and statistics in order to fit the narrative they are trying to tell. Is Namibia's education system better than it was before independence? Absolutely! But other questions cannot be answered as easily. Are learners receiving a quality education? Is Namibia getting a decent return on its investment since the country spends almost 25% of the national budget on education? What course of action should the country take from here?

The road to a successful education system in Namibia appears to be full of detours and reroutes, with many twists and turns. The condition of this educational road could aptly be likened to the actual state of the country's roadways. Some roads are well maintained while many need to be repaved, and still other areas haven't been paved at all. And then there are places where the road is impassible, and forward progress cannot be made. But regardless of the state of this educational roadway, its direction is equally important. Fittingly, the situation can be summed up with an old African proverb: If you don't know where you are going then any road will lead you there.

Chapter 10

We Are Not Understanding?

It's no secret that most Eengedjo learners had difficulty grasping parts of the English language. In trying to understand why certain problems persist, one must navigate a labyrinth of linguistic errors. Truthfully, since my experience was relegated to the small village of Omungwelume, I can't speak on behalf of the entire country. Yet from talking with the other volunteers, challenges in English seem to be a nationwide issue.

Since so much emphasis is academically placed on English, understanding the learners' mistakes becomes extremely important. For example, some mistakes are directly linked to discrepancies between the native tongue and the English language. In Oshikwanyama, the word *kwafelenge* is used to signify the English meaning of borrow/help/lend. Therefore, it is a common mistake for learners to substitute the word *help* for *lend* or *borrow*, as in "Can you help me a pencil?" In addition, there are numerous other English gaffes, inaccuracies, and idiosyncrasies that have been taught over the years and are now ingrained within the Namibian English vernacular.

One of the most discerning features of Namibian English is the constant use of appositives. An appositive is a noun or phrase that renames and modifies another noun or phrase beside it. For example: *Mr. Wes, the only oshilumbu at Eengedjo, was not accustomed to hearing people speak using appositives.* In this sentence, I identify myself and then do it again by saying I am *the only oshilumbu at Eengedjo.* But in Namibia the use of appositives became a form of redundancy. People would identify the subject with an object pronoun, and then use a subject pronoun as an appositive. Here are a few examples of what people might say:

- "Me I like to watch soccer."
- "Learners they need to study hard."
- "Mr. Wes he is good at math."

Most commonly, I would hear learners and teachers say, "Me I..." followed by some statement. Though I would constantly remind them of the awkward redundancy, this was an uphill battle since it was continuously used and reinforced every day outside of the classroom by their peers and all other adults.

People also took liberties with grammatical rules, such as using non-action verbs in the continuous tense. The continuous tense is typically used in English to describe an action that is happening at that very moment. It is formed with the verb *to be* along with the *base verb* + *–ing*. For example: I am walking to school. Typically, non-action verbs cannot be used in the continuous tense because they are words that describe conditions without action that last for a duration of time. A common example would be verbs that express emotion, feeling, or possession: *to love, to like, to have, to want, to know*. However, the learners had a difficult time distinguishing between action and non-action verbs when using the continuous tense. Often, I would hear people make comments like:

- "Me I am *wanting* a pencil."
- "Are you *owning* this book?"
- "Mr. Wes, we are *liking* your class."

I was happy the learners *were liking* my class, but such grammar missteps were frustrating. Acclimating to some cultural quirks, such as snapping in class, was no trouble. However, these distinct uses of English never got any easier on my ears, and these practices were so blatantly rampant that they must have been taught to the learners at some point during their education. Thus, the task of changing these nuances would be like a zebra trying to erase its stripes. For better or for worse, certain linguistic idiosyncrasies seem to be permanently etched into the stone of Namibian English.

Interestingly enough, these English parlances were not limited to spoken language but maintained throughout the learners' writing assignments. But believe it or not, this wasn't the strangest aspect of their writing. One facet of writing just about all learners engaged in was Short Message Service (SMS) language. Even though the vast majority of kids didn't own a cellular phone, they seemed to be well up to speed as to the shorthand of SMS, or text messaging, language. Writing assignments were rife with abbreviations, acronyms, and reductions. Most commonly, learners would write the word *you* with the letter *u*. In some instances, learners would use numbers to represent words, such as writing *today* as *2day*, or *great* as *gr8*. Some writing assignments looked like learners were sending me a long text message. The issue of SMS language in place of proper English is not only limited to Namibia but is endemic in writing among younger generations worldwide. The concern in a place like rural Namibia, however, is kids are learning SMS messaging in conjunction with learning how to write longhand English and well before learning to type on a keyboard. Therefore, it is possible that some kids will not distinguish between SMS language and standard written English. Even to this day, I have stayed in contact with former learners via social media, and just about all email messages are written using SMS language. But this was just the tip of the iceberg when it came to writing.

There were numerous writing idiosyncrasies which, once again, were probably taught at some point during the learners' education. Writing a letter was an assignment I would often give the learners since it's an exercise commonly found on national assessment exams. What struck me was the unusual greeting learners would begin their letters with. Many of them would write something like this:

> *Dear Mr. Wes,*
> *Hello! How are you? Back to me, I'm fine.*

Another interesting expression I came across dealt with the prepositional phrase *according to*. Sometimes, when learners attempted to express an argument, view, or belief, they would write:

> *According to my opinion....*

But even with the use of such atypical phrases, there was still another writing culprit I had to contend with – God.

In Namibia, there was not always separation between school and religion. Although people maintain a strong, indigenous identity, roughly 90% of all Namibians claim to be Christian. At Eengedjo, church services were held in the school's dining hall every Sunday. Even though there wasn't a policy that placed Christianity within the curriculum, learners would display their faith on their own. And they would often do so in their writing assignments.

Whenever I gave the learners a writing assignment such as an article, essay, or letter, I frequently included an assignment description and word count so learners knew how much to write. An assignment might look something like this:

> *Write an article for your school magazine about a market you visited recently. Your article should include:*
>
> - *What you saw*
> - *The best thing you saw*
> - *How you felt*

*You should write about **200 words**.*

Some learners would begin the article like so:

Lord, thank you for giving me the strength to write this article. You are the almighty. Please be with me at all times. You are the savior. And I thank you every day for all that you have given me. Please always watch over me. Guide my hand as I write this article....

Scripture such as this would go on for about 175 words, and then they would write two pithy sentences at the end about visiting a market. I had no problem with learners expressing their religious beliefs, but I did have a problem with them not completing the assignment. I would tell them it was okay if they wanted to express their faith, but it could reasonably be done in just one or two sentences. I can't profess to speak on behalf of the Almighty, but I imagine God would probably want them to answer the question.

Other common writing faux pas included basic spelling and grammar mistakes, many of which are common with English learners worldwide. The learners inevitably attempted to spell words the way they sound. Most would spell *Wednesday* the way it is pronounced, *Wensday*. Another common misspelling occurred with the word *first*, which learners would spell as *frist*. Rules of capitalization were also frequently ignored. For example, learners would forget to capitalize the first word of a sentence, or they would fail to distinguish between proper and common nouns. When writing the pronoun *I*, many learners would write the lowercase letter *i* instead, jotting down sentences like – *i study english on wensday*. Ultimately, spelling and rules of capitalization were applications that had to be reviewed and reinforced over and over again.

Punctuation was another issue. Many learners had difficulty using a full stop, which is called a *period* in American English. Essentially, learners would not use full stops and would instead combine everything with a conjunction, using *and, or, but,* or *so* in order to keep the sentences going, and going, and going. Many paragraphs were just one sentence and the style appeared polysyndenton, which is a grammar term for the use of successive conjunctions when writing text. It was as though I were reading Ernest Hemingway.

In order to address many of these issues, I would constantly have the learners writing. Just about every class, I would give them some kind of writing assignment. I also implemented the technique of peer editing, hoping learners would start to recognize the writing mistakes of their classmates, which in turn might help them recognize mistakes in their own writing. Over time, I felt the learners improved. We eliminated redundancies, corrected grammar quirks, and wrote out words in longhand. Ultimately, progress was slow. But we didn't need to move fast because speed is better suited for those who wish to go it alone. In order for us to go far, we had to move together, even if it meant progressing at the local pace of life – slow and methodical.

Lately, people are pointing fingers as to why learners have such difficulty with English. Those primarily being singled out as the problem are the teachers. In September of 2011, the MOE administered an English Proficiency Placement Test for all school principals, teachers, and student teachers at the University of Namibia, planning to use the outcome of the examination to identify further training needs. The exam tested educators on comprehension, grammar, and writing. The results were less than desirable since the average score was a paltry 59%, which the ministry deemed an intermediate level of proficiency. Only 2% of the teachers scored between 93 – 100% and were exempted from further language training. But even top-performing exam takers reportedly made simple mistakes regarding capitalization and subject-verb agreement. The media went into a frenzy, and *The Namibian* newspaper released a scathing article stating 98% of Namibian teachers cannot read, write, and speak English well enough to do their jobs. The Ministry of Education immediately dismissed the results as being misinterpreted, although many felt the government was downplaying the situation. The exam results have been followed by more calls for education reform. Some even want school children to learn in their native language and abandon the English language policy altogether. But for now, the MOE has shown no signs of entertaining such changes. Still, the country cannot settle for mediocrity, and the fact remains something must be done. Namibian learners they are needing help.

A group of young boys at Eengedjo after finishing classes for the day

Chapter 11
Namlish

Shortly after I started teaching, the rainy season fell upon us in full force. The core of the rainy season lasts from January to March. However, people don't feel the true effects until April or May, as the floodwaters from Angola rush over the border and fill the *oshanas* (the Ovambo word for flood plain). The floodwaters are as fickle as the weather. They can either benefit the region or devastate local farmlands. Typically, people anticipate the yearly floods because they bring fish, restore grazing capacity, and assure water reserves for the dry months ahead. But too much flooding does more damage than good because it may harm the lands of subsistence farmers, which is still the livelihood of many people in rural areas. Schools may also get shut down. The year before I began teaching in Namibia, a volunteer's school was closed for an entire month. That same year, in 2009, over 21,000 people in the northern region of the country were displaced due to intense flooding.

As 2010 got underway, the rains arrived late. The rainy season in general was rather mild, or so I was told. But by February, lines of dark clouds burst onto the scene on a daily basis. There was no better place to feel the intensity of the rain than from inside the classroom. Since the roof of each classroom was sheets of corrugated metal, the sound of something hitting it, even if it were a small droplet of water, would echo loudly. Once the rain started to come down, I would have to raise my voice a few notches. As the rain kept coming, the competition was on. I would try to carry on speaking, pretending to ignore the sound of falling water. But the harder the rain fell from the sky, the louder the disturbance. And one by one, the learners became distracted from the lesson.

Streams of water would flow from the roof and splash onto an already flooded courtyard. I talked louder, but when the clouds truly unleashed their full power, it ceased to be much of a competition. The learners could not hear a word I was saying. Heck, I couldn't even hear myself. We would just have to wait for the pelting sound of rain to subside.

One time, after a heavy downpour, a grade 11 learner in my English class, Walter, raised his hand.

"Mr. Wes, when the rain is raining we can't hear anything." I nodded my head in agreement.

Wait! What did he just say?

"Did you say the rain is raining?" I asked him.

"Yes, the rain is raining," he replied.

"I don't think that's right." I always tried to be diplomatic when correcting the learners' speech. Some of them were a bit sensitive since English was supposed to be one of their first languages. I told Walter, "What you mean to say is, 'It's raining'."

"Ooh, sir!" he said in mild protest. The use of *ooh* is another unique part of people's speech. It has no real meaning, but is frequently used at the beginning of a sentence as a spoken interjection. It reminded me of the way Canadians say *eh* quite often. The sound people make when saying *ooh* is somewhat similar to saying the letter *O*, except the sound is produced in the back of the mouth and is released with a burst of air. I would hear both learners and teachers say it all the time, even when speaking Oshikwanyama. At first, it sounded strange, but I eventually got used to it. Truthfully, there was no choice in the matter.

"I think it is you who is wrong, sir," Walter continued the debate. "In Namibia, we say the rain is raining." Other students confirmed Walter's assertion. To them, the rain was, in fact, raining.

The learners became more active and interested in the discussion because my authority of English was being questioned. More people rallied to Walter's side with similar comments.

"Of course the rain is raining."

"Look at what the rain is doing now – raining!"

"Ooh, Mr. Wes! How can the rain not be raining?"

It was 43 against one. Therefore, I didn't stand much of a chance. Worse yet, I was caught so off guard I couldn't explain why it was improper English. In three years of teaching, I had never been asked to provide an explanation for this. As far as I knew, native English speakers always say, "It's raining."

The pronoun *it* is a gender-neutral singular pronoun that can be used to describe any physical or physiological subject and/or object. According to *it*'s Wikipedia page – that's right, I'm citing an open-source reference – the pronoun also serves as a place-holder subject in sentences with no identifiable actor. In this case, the pronoun *it* is called a dummy pronoun, whereas *it* does not refer to any particular agent. An example sentence of this use would be – drum roll, please – *It is raining.*

At the time, I was the one who looked like a dummy because I had no idea that a dummy pronoun even existed. I asked the learners if they thought it's possible in other cases as well, such as saying, *"The snow is snowing."* Appropriately, I received this response: "Ooh, Mr. Wes, we have never seen snow. So how can we know if the snow is snowing? But I'm looking at the rain raining right now." Who could fault them for this logic? Empirical evidence is often the best way to formulate one's thoughts and opinions. But English grammar is fact, not opinion. Or is it?

This was my introduction to a completely different usage of the English language, and there was much more to come. I discovered numerous differences in both pronunciation and vocabulary, which often caused great confusion. Who's to say exactly where, and to what extent, an imperialist form of *proper English* should extend its authority? Arguably, one could say some areas are asking for English autonomy. In many ways, it seems as if proper English is powerless because even in remote places like Omungwelume, the rain is raining on its parade.

Determining where to take a stand on proper English was a challenge, and trying to roll back some grammatical gaffes seemed insurmountable. Many of my grade 11 learners were already in their 20s, and they weren't as impressionable as some of the younger kids. It made me wonder if Namibian English were truly just a different dialect of English. But determining some of the differences between American English, British English, and Namibian English was another challenge altogether. Sometimes I wasn't sure which I was dealing with, and at times, it wasn't so obvious.

"**Mr.** Wes, can you help me with a science problem?" a colleague asked me one day in the staffroom. Questions such as this were common. Since I was a foreigner with an education from a Western university, many people assumed I had a working knowledge of just about every field of study. No matter what the topic – the use of recycled plastic drums, compound molecules, even floral arrangements – I would get riddled with questions, even though anyone else's guess was as good as mine.

"Do you know much about ar-yoo-minium?" my colleague asked.

"I'm sorry, what did you say?"

"Aryoominium," my colleague repeated. "Do you know much about it?"

"I can't really say that I do," I confessed. "What is aryoominium?" My colleague looked astonished at my ignorance.

"Ooh, you don't know aryoominium?" he said, and chuckled to himself. "How is this possible? He paused and began sorting through a clutter of stuff on the table, presumably in search of this elusive material. "Ah hah," he shouted. He grabbed something from behind a stack of papers. Namibia is home to an abundance of exquisite minerals, so at this point I was very curious.

My colleague triumphantly held up a can of Sprite and proclaimed, "Aryoominium!"

My heightened sense of anticipation deflated and confusion set in. I was well aware of the existence of a can of Sprite, but slowly the pieces started to come together.

"Do you mean aluminum?" I asked.

"No Mr. Wes. This is aryoominium."

"Aluminum!"

"Aryoominium!"

We went back and forth in violent agreement as to what the can was made of, until finally it became clear we were talking about the same thing. We just pronounced the word *aluminum* differently. To me, aryoominium sounded about as strange as a lion eating grass. But for the most part, there was a logical explanation for this pronunciation discrepancy.

In English, there are actually two different ways to spell the 13th element of the periodic table. *Aluminum* is the American spelling, and *Aluminium* is the British spelling. Humphery Davy was a chemist in the early 1800s first credited with isolating the properties of this metal, which he called aluminum. However, given that other elements discovered at the time all carried the *–ium* suffix – potassium, magnesium, sodium – it was added to *aluminum*, therefore becoming *aluminium*. But it was Charles Martin Hall, a man who discovered a new electrolytic method of producing the metal, who is credited with popularizing the spelling *aluminum* in the United States, even though the rest of the English-speaking world spells it *aluminium*.

This explained only part of our *aluminum/aluminium* confusion. Apart from differences between American and British English, my colleague threw me off with the R/L pronunciation. The enunciation of these two letters challenged many of the learners at Eengedjo, and even some of the teachers. The end result was a failure to communicate, even though we were referring to the same metal.[5] When I told some of my classes about this pronunciation confusion the next day, many of the learners laughed at the way I said aluminum. They thought it was hilarious.

"Say it again, sir," they insisted. "That's very funny."

Perhaps I'm the lion eating the grass?

Even after I gave the learners a little history behind aluminum's etymology, they were still convinced my pronunciation was wrong. This incident made me realize that I would have to be vigilant about the different varieties of English, apart from spelling differences like *color* and *colour*, or *favorite* and *favourite*. Word choice was also the cause of some confusion on my part. This is another area where American and British English have been known to diverge. I realized this one day when I gave a quiz to my grade 9 math class. After handing out the quiz, which dealt with basic algebra, one girl named Johanna raised her hand. I walked over to her so I could hear her question. When I was next to her desk, she looked up at me imploringly.

"Sir, can you help me a rubber?" I gave her a peculiar look. One might think her choice of verbs was the reason why the question was so baffling. But that wasn't it.

"You need what?" I asked, seemingly nonplussed.

She attempted to correct herself. "Sorry, sir. Can you borrow me a rubber?"

The words *lend* and *borrow* were frequently misused. However, this didn't ameliorate my confusion.

A rubber is American slang for a condom. And for the life of me, I couldn't figure out why she would ask me for a condom in the middle of a math quiz. I knew that schools throughout Namibia

---

[5] FYI – my colleagues' question referred to a science problem that involved the number of isotopes aluminum has. I wasn't much help, but together we managed to find the solution. At least I think so.

greatly promoted the use of contraceptives given high HIV rates, but now wasn't the time, was it?

"Johanna, I don't think we should discuss this." Now it was Johanna's turn to look confused.

"Ooh, but sir, I need a rubber," she repeated.

"Johanna, just finish your math quiz." At this point another learner, who had overheard our conversation, turned around and placed an eraser on the corner of Johanna's desk. She grabbed the eraser, smiled at me, and then proceeded to erase one of her answers.

Gee, Mr. Wes. You're such an idiot.

In the beginning, I really had to learn some of the distinctions between American and British English. The *bathroom* was the *toilet*. *Pants* were *trousers*. *Chips* were *crisps*. And *erasers* were apparently *rubbers*. These differences sometimes hindered communication, although the real challenge was with the linguistic varieties of Namibian English. As soon as I arrived, I was introduced to the world of Namlish.

Given the global prominence of the English language, it has inevitably fused with other native languages where it is being taught or spoken. The outcome of this language blending sometimes results in a unique variance of the two languages. English has many varieties such as this, whose names form a portmanteau: *Chinglish* (English-Chinese), *Spanglish* (English-Spanish), *Runglish* (English-Russian), *Japanglish* (English-Japanese), *Konglish* (English-Korean), *Dunglish* (English-Danish). When I arrived in Namibia, I quickly learned about the country's own linguistic variety known as *Namlish*.

Namlish, sometimes called Namblish, is a portmanteau of the words English and Namibia. Of course Namibia is a country and not a language, however Namlish has been derived from the blending of English with many of the country's different tribal languages. Even though English is the official language of Namibia, it is actually the second or third language for many Namibian residents. Therefore, Namlish is a unique version of English, which is communicated daily using different vocabulary, expressions, and nuances.

Distinguishing Namlish from English was easy at times, simply because I had never heard the words before. Take the word *truck*, for example, which in British English is called a *lorry*. In Namibia, most people refer to a tuck as a *bakkie*. Same goes for the word *bar*, which is referred to as a *pub* in British English and a *shabeen* in Namlish. If a person decides to drink a lot at a shabeen, they may feel *bubbulas* the next morning which is the Namlish word for *hung-over*. At Eengedjo, it wasn't long before I heard the word *tuckshop*, which is a small school shop that sells supplies and snack food. Even though some of the terms seemed strange, these new vocabulary words didn't cause any misunderstandings. Namlish caused the most confusion with words I already knew.

After my first term of teaching, I traveled to Windhoek with a friend, where we planned to rendezvous with a few other volunteers before continuing on to Cape Town, South Africa. While waiting in Windhoek, my friend and I went shopping. At one point, we ended up getting turned around and had to ask a gentleman for help. The man said he knew the street we were looking for and then gave us directions.

"Follow the robots down this street. Take a left at the third robot, and follow it for one more robot."

I looked at my friend who also seemed confused. Unwilling to openly confess to our ignorance, we thanked the man and kept walking.

"Do you know what he was talking about?" I asked.

After thinking about it, she said, "Maybe he was talking about the traffic lights." Now the directions made a bit more sense. In Namibia, traffic lights are commonly referred to as *robots*. I don't know why; they just are.

There is an assortment of words, such as *robots*, commonly used in American and British English that have taken on a different meaning in Namlish. Sometimes, I would hear the learners accusing each other of *puffing*, which I thought meant smoking. Then one time in class a learner blurted out, "Who puffed?" Since the comment was starting to distract learners from the lesson, I told them it was me so we could move on. My confession was accompanied by several snickers. Afterwards, I learned that *puff* means *fart*. I would also hear the term *small boy* quite often, which I initially equated to a person's size and stature. However, in Namlish, a *small boy* generally refers to a young, unmarried man. How about a *stiffy*? Can you guess what that is? A *stiffy* is Namlish for a 3 ½" floppy computer disk. It's an unusual term, but what was even more unusual was that many computers in Namibia could still take a 3 ½" floppy disk. Another word I would frequently hear, but often in a derogatory sense, was *villager*. A *villager*, not surprisingly, is a person from a village. But it's used to describe a person who is uneducated, uncouth, or uncivilized. Often the kids would tease one another by calling each other *villagers*. Some other Namlish vocabulary: a *cool drink* means soda, *hot stuff* means hard liquor, *soapie* means a TV soap opera, to *fall pregnant* means an accidental pregnancy, and to *hold thumbs* means to keep your fingers crossed for good luck. Even though I was the person teaching English, it immediately became apparent that I wasn't the only one who would be learning it.

Finally, there is Namlish which transcends beyond accepted proper English. This form of Namlish is perhaps the most fascinating, such as the use of *now*. Never would I have guessed that the word *now* would mean *later*. Or that *now now* would mean *soon*, and *now now now* would actually mean...*now*. Sometimes, when I wanted to stress urgency to the learners I would say *now* about a dozen times to reinforce timeliness.

Overall, I just had to adjust my ears to hearing remarks such as "The rain is raining." Or listen to learners constantly ask me, "Mr.

Wes, help me a pencil!" I'm just glad nobody asked me when I first arrived, "Mr. Wes, help me a stiffy." I may have gotten worried. Yet just like so many other dialects of English around the world, Namlish may be here to stay. It's now a living language that is spreading, adapting, and evolving. Namlish is even fusing together with other English dialects in Southern Africa. Thus, we should probably acknowledge that English is constantly changing, in Namibia, and across the globe. And as of right now now now, we should maintain serenity in accepting that this is something which may not change.

Chapter 12
Unnatural Resources

"In Africa, we share."

This is a statement I heard on numerous occasions. And it's true, especially in areas where resources are scarce. The benevolent notion of sharing – "What's mine is yours, and what's yours is mine." – goes a long way in impoverished communities. Sharing becomes integrated with daily survival. The learners at Eengedjo would share just about everything – pencils, erasers (rubbers), notebooks, chairs, desks, and unfortunately even their homework assignments. But as I stood there looking over this group of learners who had three different sets of hands laid across the computer keyboard, I tried to think of a way to tell them sharing is not always an option. However, instead of explaining it, I tried to show them.

I moved their hands away from the keyboard and leaned over the three learners who were crammed onto a single chair in front of the computer. I placed my fingers over the home keys to show them how their fingers should be aligned. I then asked the learners to say something, which initially confused them but eventually we started conversing. As we spoke, I began transcribing the conversation, which started to appear on the computer screen. When the learners realized I was typing out our conversation in real-time, they were utterly amazed, as if it were some type of illusion.

"Mr. Wes, I want to type like you," they said. "Teach me!"

Unfortunately, this was easier said than done. What frustrated me about teaching computers was that the longer I taught the subject, the more I felt it was an exercise in futility. On several occasions, the thought of giving up crossed my mind. But I was determined to keep moving forward, even if at a snail's pace, until every last computer was officially declared…deceased.

The first time I ever used a computer in school was in the 9th grade. Every student in the class was able to operate their own computer. Most lessons centered on learning how to type. For three months, I practiced on the computer's typing program for 50 minutes, three times a week. Gradually, the rate at which I could type grew exponentially from 10 words a minute, to 25 words a minute, to over 40 words a minute. At the time, I didn't realize computers would soon dominate our lives. Yet my ability to learn had nothing to do with special skills I possessed. It had everything to do with the fact that I had the resource of a computer at my disposal.

At Eengedjo, I taught computer skills to all six of the grade 12 classes. The learners had class once during their seven-day scheduled week, which meant I wouldn't even see all six classes each week. On average, there were about 40 learners per class and only seven functioning computers. Thus, teaching them to type was like teaching 40 kids to write with only seven pencils. But let's do the math! Usually the learner-to-computer ratio was about 6:1. In a 45-minute class, each learner would get to use the computer for approximately 7 ½ minutes. Over 15 years ago, my high school in the U.S. provided me with 150 minutes a week on the computer. Talk about a discrepancy in resources! I couldn't help but wonder what the learning curve is for someone who has access to computers for only 7 ½ minutes per week.

When I first entered the computer room – just after the alarm had sounded – I started having qualms about this teaching endeavor. There were 10 old IBM computers stationed on two different round wooden tables. I was overcome with a feeling of nostalgic trepidation. The nostalgia came from the memory of the very first computer my family had bought back in the late 80s. This also caused trepidation because, in the new millennium, these computers were dinosaurs of technology.

As I walked around the dusty room, I hit the power button on each computer. I was amazed to find most of them still operated. All of them ran off of a single server, an IBM computer in the corner of the room which was the newest computer at around 10 years old. If this computer crashed, or was shut down, then none of the others would operate. The computers ran on an operating system called Edubuntu, which is a form of Linux specifically designed for school use. In order to gain access to the server, a login and password were required, and that information was taped to the top of each monitor. In the corner of the room, I found several cardboard boxes containing old computer parts, such as keyboards, CPU units, monitors, and several mouse devices. Over time, I tested the parts only to reconfirm their lack of functionality. But they made great visual aids in the classroom, and we began with that.

As the course got underway, I brought in the box of parts to start the learners out with some basic computer vocabulary. We also talked about turning the computer on and off, how to use the mouse, and where to position fingers on the keyboard. I even had the learners draw a keyboard on a piece of paper so they could practice typing. After a couple of weeks, I took them to the computer room and we tried to put theory into practice.

When the course began, I discovered many of the learners in grade 12 had never used a computer. They didn't have one at home, and small villages are not typically equipped with an Internet café. Thus, kids weren't ordering items off of Amazon, streaming YouTube videos, or tweeting about the trees they were sitting under. But all this was about to change. People in rural communities are thirsty to access cyberspace, and in 2010, I was the person who would light their way into the world of computers. Except with the computers we had at our disposal, I would be leading the way with a pack of matches instead of a torch.

The school's computer room

Teaching computer skills slowly became a thorn in my side. I would get frustrated because often I felt the learners wouldn't listen to the instructions. In order to save time, since the computers took about five minutes to boot up, I would go ahead and turn them on. The learners would just need to log in. I would tell them the computers were already on and would even make them verbally repeat this information. But as soon as we got to the computer room, learners instinctively hit the power button and turned the computer off. If this happened to the network computer, all the computers would have to be restarted. It could easily turn a 45-minute class into a 30-minute class. At times, it was exasperating having to constantly reiterate basic operations. I was reminded of a teaching aphorism I once heard – *A great teacher always says things more than once.*

The learners can't shoulder all the responsibility. I also got irritated at my own shortcomings as an instructor. For our limited resources, I was moving entirely too fast. I tried to cover a lesson on the mouse in one class – how to hold the mouse, left click, right click, and double-click. Yet mastery of these techniques required several lessons in the computer room. After a while, I had to hit my brain's "ctrl-alt-delete" button to restart my expectations. I slowed down the pace of the lessons, and we took our time learning each operation. As much as I tried to emphasize typing, the truth of the matter was that most of the kids weren't going to learn how to type. In fact, very few of them would even get their foot in the door. This wasn't anyone's fault. It was just the reality of our situation.

Dealing with the computers themselves was perhaps the most maddening part of it all. The electrical supply throughout Omungwelume was erratic. Electrical spikes, blackouts, and brownouts were common occurrences, and the computers had no surge protector. Any sort of power disruption whatsoever would send our dinosaurs into a tizzy. Thus, the number of functioning computers remained cyclical throughout the year. On average, out of the 10 computers in the room, only about six or seven would work on any given day. Some days, I would try to turn on the computers and nothing would work at all.

Although the learners and I both showed a certain level of incompetence when it came to our computer course, it was the lack of computers that truly diminished my spirits. This was a perfect example of too many kids and too few resources. But the government is trying to address this issue. Since 2010, the MOE has been in the process of providing schools with new computers. The stipulation, however, is schools must implement computer classes into their curriculum. Many schools are taking advantage of this program, but it takes time to get classes set up. At the school of one WorldTeach volunteer, there were over a dozen brand new computers sitting in boxes. Still, other volunteers had no computer resources at all.

Before coming to Namibia, I had never been placed in an instructional capacity where resources were few. Over the long run, it made me appreciate what we had, but most importantly it made me adjust my approach to teaching. Truthfully, if I could do it all over again, I would have changed much of the curriculum in my computer class. But I learned from my mistakes, and this is how education should work. We should learn from the past in order to effectively focus on the future.

In developed countries, it's easy for people to take conveniences for granted. Sometimes the notion of living without amenities and luxuries is even romanticized. I remember writing an email to a friend about the lack of resources available to me at school. Perhaps I was being a bit down on my situation and unnecessarily using this person as a sounding board. My friend promptly responded with a bit of hopeful optimism, but at the time I was in no mood for a quote by Sheryl Crow – "It's not having what you want. It's wanting what you've got." At Eengedjo, I often felt it wasn't necessarily about having what we wanted, but about having what we needed.

When I taught in South Korea, I didn't fully appreciate a lot of the school amenities available to me – markers, pens, books, paper, and a copy machine I could use for unlimited copies. If a learner asked me a question I couldn't answer, I had a computer with internet access right there in the classroom. The learners were also aptly prepared with pencils, notebooks, textbooks, calculators, rulers...everything they needed for their studies. Eengedjo was a whole new ball game. It's like we were trying to play the game, just without the proper equipment.

Without a doubt, the greatest resource in the classroom is the teacher. Teachers are the ultimate facilitators of knowledge and information. But without adequate resources, teachers really have to think outside the box. I had to plan my lessons around the contingency that certain amenities might not be available, such as electricity to make copies, show a video, or use the computers. I would even have to use chalk sparingly. Still, the show must go on, even if the lack of resources affects the show's performance.

The bottom line is that the resource discrepancy between certain countries is overwhelming, and places like Omungwelume find themselves in a bit of quagmire. The lack of resources, such as textbooks, chairs, desks, and even teachers greatly slows the rate of learning. On the other side of the spectrum, some classrooms in developed countries are getting equipped with SMART Boards, which are multi-media whiteboards that allow teachers to integrate the Internet, pictures, or videos into their lessons. So how are countries that are academically behind supposed to catch up to modern contemporaries while moving at a slower pace?

One of the biggest challenges the school faced when it came to resources was the lack of sufficient chairs and desks. This shortage inevitably caused some learners to stand in class, which never bothered me, but I did notice a difference between the effort put forth by those learners who were sitting and those standing. By far the most productive classes were when everyone had a chair to sit in and a desk to write on, which wasn't usually the case.

The school was not the only one short on supplies. The learners lacked many basic materials like pens and pencils. Other supplies, such as calculators, were a hot commodity because most learners claimed they couldn't afford one. Throughout the year, my family would periodically ship packages to me containing packets of pens, pencils, rulers and other school supplies. I would unload these materials on the kids as rewards, or if they needed to borrow something during a lesson. Yet deficiencies remained, and the end result was everyone just had to share.

All the aforementioned are material challenges rural Namibia faces – lack of computers, textbooks, chairs, and desks. Yet this just scratches the surface when it comes to the country's shortage of educational resources. According to an article in *The Namibian*, the MOE has claimed the country will have a huge shortage of teachers between 2012 and 2015. They estimate during this time there will be a shortfall of roughly 3,000 primary school teachers and 2,000 secondary school teachers. There is also the financial challenge of funding education. Namibia pours roughly one-fourth of its national budget into education, but one could argue it's still not enough since many schools are badly in need of renovations and a growing number of learners are calling for financial assistance. But some improvements have been made such as the construction of new schools which offer more access to public education. The year after I left, I was told major renovations took place at Eengedjo. Classroom roofs were replaced, buildings were repainted, and windows and doors were repaired. Yet, are such improvements keeping pace with the rest of the world?

Before leaving Eengedjo, we had a staff meeting about the school budget for the following year. Each department pleaded its case for additional finances and how they would be used. Since my computer class was a non-promotional subject, it didn't fall within any one department. Therefore, I made a plea to the principal and the other staff members for new computers. However, that plea may have fallen on deaf ears. As far as I know, Eengedjo is still without new computers and the existing computers have all stopped working.

As much as I could go on about the deficiency of resources at Eengedjo, other schools face even greater challenges. At one volunteer's location, he taught at a hostel school without a hostel. The kids lived in tents on the school grounds. Many schools face teacher shortages, and when there are not enough teachers, the learners may not always be learning. Even with such dire situations, the learners who attend classes on a regular basis are a true testament to young children doing whatever they can to create a brighter future for themselves. People have told me what I was doing as a volunteer teacher was inspirational. However, what I was doing pales in comparison to what these kids are attempting. They are trying to receive an education, even in the face of unfavorable circumstances. They are the very definition of inspiration.

A group of learners using a typing program

Chapter 13

Mr. Wes' Ghost

Corporal punishment is illegal in Namibia's schools. Article 56 (1) of the Education Act of 2001 prohibits any teacher or person employed at a private or public school to administer corporal punishment upon any learner. Although this is guaranteed in writing, some people contend the practice of corporal punishment is still alive and well. But why use such force in the education system? The school of thought behind utilizing corporal punishment is to cause pain, but not injury, in order to correct, control, or modify behavior. Many attempts have been made by researchers to distinguish the dividing line between physical punishment and physical abuse, but there is no general agreement. Basically, is there any way to define what a "safe smack" is?

Discipline helps guide our moral compass. If we do something morally objectionable, we may likely be disciplined for it. The goal, however, is for us to learn from being disciplined so the immoral act will no longer be committed. This is considered positive discipline. Negative discipline, on the other hand, focuses on doing what you are told so you can avoid an unpleasant experience. Therefore, it is universally accepted that any sort of physical punishment is a form of negative discipline.

Throughout the year, I heard stories of corporal punishment. And even though our principal, Mr. Joseph, would constantly read memorandums from the MOE during staff meetings reiterating that corporal punishment should not be used, I did witness acts of physical punishment at Eengedjo. The times I witnessed physical punishment was by an older female teacher. She was actually an ordained minister and would lead the school's church sermons on Sunday. Every now and then, I would see learners enter the staffroom and walk over to where she sat. The learners would hold out one hand flat, with their palm facing down. My colleague would smack the top of their hand with a 12″ wooden ruler. It didn't seem to cause the learners bodily harm, and they probably suffered more from embarrassment than physical pain since this spectacle took place in front of the other teachers. No one at the school brought forth allegations of abuse. I also didn't rock the boat, until one day when I got involved. I stopped a boy who was leaving the staffroom after getting smacked on the hand. Apparently he had been caught helping someone cheat.

"Did that hurt?" I asked.

"No, sir," he said with a smile. "You can try," he suggested.

Being a curious individual, I asked my colleague if she would give me a whack on the hand. She laughed but obliged.

"Don't hold back," I told her.

I held out my hand and she gave it a good whack with the ruler. It made a nice sound but inflicted little physical pain. I told my colleague it didn't really hurt, so I asked why bother doing it. She told me it was to remind the learners who was in charge. Since she was not causing the learners much physical pain, I saw no need to debate her logic and escalate this issue.

Other times, I only witnessed the threat of corporal punishment because some of the teachers who administered the evening study would walk around with a yardstick. But to my knowledge, there were no major grievances about physical punishment occurring at Eengedjo. Maybe I was being naïve? Perhaps corporal punishment only happened behind closed doors? Or maybe Eengedjo didn't engage in such practices. However, there were other schools that did. Several of my fellow volunteers witnessed more extreme forms of corporal punishment than just a smack on the hand. The truth of the matter is that some schools have blatantly turned a blind eye to the issue.

So why shouldn't we use corporal punishment? Dr. Elizabeth Gershoff, a prominent researcher on disciplining children, suggests corporal punishment does not necessarily produce its desirable behavior, which is immediate compliance. She cites evidence that corporal punishment is linked to detrimental physical and emotional problems. Children who are subjected to physical punishment are more likely to become aggressive and defiant. They are also at-risk for increased anti-social behavior and mental problems. But should other factors also influence our view of corporal punishment? Should age, gender, society, or cultural norms be taken into consideration? Is there a difference between physically punishing a five-year-old and physically punishing a twenty-year-old? Or should that even matter?

I'm not a child specialist or psychologist. I also don't have any concrete answers in regard to corporal punishment, only opinions. I'm just a teacher who tries to be a good role model. And of course, a good role model would never hit another person. Truthfully though, there have been kids whom I've mentally envisioned strangling like Homer would do to Bart in *The Simpsons*. But I am above childish cartoon antics. I would never harm a child. Or would I? I thought I would be the last person to engage in some form of corporal punishment. That is, until it happened.

Since I didn't have a television to senselessly occupy my free time, I would read a lot. I know I'm probably in the minority when I say this, but I prefer nonfiction over fiction and find real life more fascinating than the imagination. I also enjoy reading about places I'm living in or traveling around. Many of my reading selections while in Namibia were books about Africa. During the second term of classes, I was immersed in reading *King Leopold's Ghost* by Adam Hochschild.

King Leopold's Ghost is the gruesome tale of the exploits of the Congo Free State by King Leopold II of Belgium. The book details some of the heinous crimes committed by European colonizers between 1885 and 1908. By means of duplicity, King Leopold colonized the Congo in order to extract the region's rubber, which was highly desirable at the time. Estimates suggest that nearly half of the Congo's population perished during Leopold's reign. Although the true number will never be known, it is believed around 10 million lives were lost. This is one of the most atrocious genocides in world history, and some people place Leopold as one of the greatest tyrants the world has ever known. But King Leopold himself never physically committed the act of murder. Yet he is held responsible and justifiably so.

Early one evening, I sat on my front porch with a glass of wine. The sun was going down and the school grounds in front of my house were deserted. All the learners were in the dining hall eating dinner. It was a peaceful evening, and I sat down to unwind with my book. I had just started a chapter called "Where There Aren't No Ten Commandments", which detailed some of the abuses Belgian soldiers committed against the indigenous populations for their noncompliance. They forced the Congolese to work and would frequently punish them with a whip called a *chicotte*.

> …a whip of raw, sun-dried hippopotamus hide, cut into a long sharp-edged corkscrew strip. Usually the chicotte was applied to the victim's bare buttocks. Its blows would leave permanent scars; more than twenty-five strokes could mean unconsciousness; and a hundred or more – not an uncommon punishment – were often fatal.

As I read the chapter, my mind began backtracking through the day's earlier events. Gradually, something became evident.

What made it possible for the functionaries in the Congo to so blithely watch the chicotte in action and, as we shall see, to deal out pain and death in other ways as well?

In such a regime, one thing that often helps functionaries 'become used to it' is a slight, symbolic distance – irrelevant to the victim – between the official in charge and the physical act of terror itself.

Although some whites in the Congo enjoyed wielding the chicotte, most put a similar symbolic distance between themselves and the dreaded instrument.

And so the bulk of chicotte blows were inflicted by Africans on bodies of other Africans.

After I read this, my attention wandered away from the book as I stared up at the passive evening skies. Then suddenly, a thought viciously hit me with the severity of the *chicotte*. The reality of my transgressions cut deep.

Oh SHIT! I just hit that kid.

Discipline at Eengedjo was never much of a problem. The learners were not overly defiant, and there wasn't much in the way of rambunctious troublemakers. The learners would, however, succumb to lethargy and exhibit a high level of indifference. The main enemy among teachers was learner apathy, which materialized for various reasons – consistently receiving bad marks, lack of job prospects, and no financial resources for higher education. So how do you combat learner apathy?

What makes kids interested in a lesson is how the material is presented. I did my best to entertain the learners with each lesson. I would use a range of intonations, I would sing, I would dance, and I would do whatever it took to maintain their attention. I believe most learners appreciated my efforts and responded with a willingness to learn. However, on occasion, learners would hit the snooze button and take a nap during my lessons.

For some reason, I took it personally when the kids slept in class. Unfortunately for those dreamers, I wasn't going to take it easy on them. While teaching, I would spend a fair amount of time roaming around the classroom. This created a more responsive audience, and I patrolled the aisles to make sure everyone was on task. I also moved about as part of habit rather than necessity, since it kept me from getting bored with some of my own grammar lessons. Usually, if a learner had their head down on a desk, I would tap one leg of the desk with my foot. The jolt was always enough to grab the learner's attention and they would raise their head. But sometimes, my maneuverability in the classroom was limited. Due to the number of learners, I couldn't readily walk around some of the smaller classrooms because the area would be cluttered with people. So how do you get to those who are out of arm's reach? Well, you have someone else do it for you.

Earlier in the day, well before I sat outside with my book and glass of wine, I had a lesson with my 11C English class. It was a riveting lesson on the Passive vs. Active Voice. Here's a simple explanation: in active voice, the subject is doing the action – "Mr. Wes teaches English." In passive voice, the target of the action, English, becomes the primary subject, and the verb *to be* is used along with the past participle of the verb *teach* – "English is taught by Mr. Wes."

Okay, to the learners' credit, the lesson may have been worthy of a mid-morning siesta. And as I blabbed on about active and passive sentences, I noticed a boy in the back of the room whose head had been down since the beginning of class. There was a crowd of learners between us so I couldn't easily get back there to wake him up.

"Cornelius!" I shouted, to which there was no response.

I said the boy's name again, louder. "CORNELIUS!"

All the learners looked back at Cornelius' corpse-like body. I broke off a small piece of chalk and lobbed it towards the back of the classroom. Sometimes I did this when I couldn't reach those deep sleepers. Usually, I was a decent shot with the chalk, but I missed and it bounced off the side of the desk. Some of the learners chuckled as Cornelius remained in a catatonic state. Another boy sitting next to him, Hango, gave him a slight shake. Still…nothing.

"Is he alive?" I asked Hango, who leaned down closer to Cornelius.

"He's not breathing," Hango said with a concerned look. My heart skipped a beat. Then Hango's smile revealed he was kidding. "He's alive. He's just a lazy villager, Mr. Wes." The other learners laughed.

I told Hango to wake him up, and he shook Cornelius back to consciousness. Cornelius came to with a big yawn. I asked if he was sick, and he assured me he wasn't. I told him to pay attention, and he sat up in his chair, opened his notebook, and began copying down the example sentences I had written on the board. Ten minutes later, Cornelius had his head back on the desk and was fast asleep.

I looked at Hango, and made a slight slapping motion with my hand. All I really wanted Hango to do was wake the boy up. He graciously obliged but interpreted my gesture as carte blanche to **really** get Cornelius' attention. Hango took the palm of his hand and smacked Cornelius hard across the back of his head. The hit made a loud thud, and some of the learners were laughing as Cornelius bolted upright. He was furious and glared at Hango who vehemently waved his hands like it wasn't his fault. He pulled away from Cornelius while pointing at me.

"Mr. Wes told me to," he pleaded to Cornelius, who turned his anger towards me.

"Hango, what the hell was that?" I yelled. "That's not what I told you."

It's what I gestured.

Still, I was the instigator, even if it were not what I intended. If I hadn't made the gesture, Hango never would have hit Cornelius. Thankfully, the situation didn't escalate. I carried on with the lesson, and Cornelius didn't go back to sleep.

After reading that chapter in *King Leopold's Ghost*, I reconsidered my actions in the classroom. This wasn't the first time I had gestured at learners to wake up their peers. Usually, the learners would just tap one another, but sometimes they would give their friends a slight smack just to mess with them. Even though Hango and Cornelius were friends, this was taken to a whole new level. Either way, I never considered that I was ultimately the one responsible for hitting the learners. Mentally, I was able to create a symbolic distance between the kids hitting one another on my behalf and the physical act itself. I was finally able to see the parallels while reading about the atrocious crimes in the Congo. Arguably, one could say I was implementing a form of corporal punishment. Suffice it to say, that was the last time I asked a learner to wake up one of their peers.

Corporal punishment is an issue that may always be debated within education systems worldwide. There is a common argument people use when it comes to physical punishment: "I was disciplined physically when I was a child, and I turned out to be a well-behaved, polite, nice person." In my own case, there is truth to this. As I child, if I misbehaved, I was occasionally spanked. Frankly, I deserved it. Granted, this was back in the 80s, and views on parenting were completely different. But what were the results? Did this punishment truly alter my behavior? Probably not. Did it fill me with emotional resentment? I don't think so. It probably had little effect at all. But the fact that it did not affect me could be a reason I am more complacent with physical punishment. It becomes easy to develop a mentality of "What works for me should work for others." But what we should really take into consideration is this: "What did not affect me could possibly affect someone else."

The problem with corporal punishment is there is no definitive line between abuse and punishment. And the lack of being able to define such a line is justification to not implement corporal punishment. Overall, I think Western eyes are perhaps a bit more sensitive when it comes to this issues. And the fact that corporal punishment endures in Namibia leads me to believe society is tolerant with certain levels of it. When I witnessed the learners getting smacked with the ruler, I didn't consider that abuse. However, another person might. School learners should be protected, but they should also respect authority. And that's the tricky part. Either way, if teachers are going to discipline learners, then they should do it themselves. At least then they will consciously be accountable for the punishment.

Chapter 14
The Nonsocial Butterfly

The word *friend* can imply a varying of degrees. If used with an adjective, we can modify the noun more precisely, such as with *good friend, close friend, old friend,* or *best friend*. In Omungwelume, I didn't consider anyone to be a "good friend." My social life, to be perfectly honest, was rather dismal. I wasn't necessarily a loner, but I would categorize my friends into three types: *colleague friends, learner friends,* and *imaginary friends*.

At Eengedjo, I was one of five teachers who lived on school property, although the other teachers also worked as hostel supervisors. Most of the teaching staff lived just outside the school gates in government-provided housing. In their free time, everyone more or less maintained a life outside of school, and on the weekends most would return to their hometowns. A good number of the school staff were older men and women who had families. Some of the younger female teachers, although they weren't married, also had children. There were a few younger male colleagues who were around my age, and on occasion I would hang out with them. But our options for hanging out were limited, and it usually involved drinking at one of Omungwelume's many shabeens.

When I think of the bar scene, it is a social gathering, especially between opposite sexes. Shabeens are quite the contrary and, for the most part, are male-dominated. Of course, there are some women at shabeens, but they usually work there. Thus, shabeens are predominantly full of belligerent men dancing by themselves.

Carrying on a conversation in a shabeen can be an annoying task. The music is so loud that people have to yell. It is one of those places where the social protocol is to sit and nod politely. Whenever I went to a shabeen, I often listened to the same songs over and over and over. Namibians have a strong tolerance for repetition, and the hit song when I first arrived was DJ Bojo Mojo's, *Marry Me*. It is probably the song I have heard more than any other in my entire life.

My closest colleague friend was a guy named Hendrick, who was a math teacher about my age. He was always well-dressed for work, wearing nice buttoned-up shirts, khakis, and colorful neckties that looked peculiar because they were so short they didn't even reach down to his stomach. Yet short ties like this were stylish in Namibia, even if I did think they looked a bit goofy. Hendrick was very ambitious and well-spoken. I had no doubt he would become a school principal someday. On occasion, I would go with Hendrick to the shabeens in Omungwelume or travel with him to Oshakati, which offered a more lively nightlife. It was nice to socialize, but this really wasn't my kind of scene.

By far, the most enjoyable social environment was drinking marula juice after school. The marula tree is indigenous to Southern Africa and bears a small, round, yellowish fruit typically harvested from January to March when it falls to the ground. The pulp of the marula fruit is used to make juices, jams, jellies, and an alcoholic drink commonly known as marula juice. The juice is made by extracting the juices from the fruit and allowing the liquid to run through a sieve. It's fermented for a few days and then bottled in a container. People told me marula juice contains anywhere from 3 – 20% alcohol, but it's really hard to say because there's not much quality control when producing these homemade batches. The drink tastes a bit pungent, but it's commonly mixed with soda to lessen the bite. Drinking marula juice is a social pastime among Ovambos. People sit around in groups to converse and share stories while enjoying a jug of freshly made marula juice. It's an Ovambo-style happy hour, at least for several months during the marula season.

During February, March, and April, the marjula juice season was in full bloom, and I would go drink with some of my colleagues once or twice a week. I've never shied away from participating in different customs, especially those that involve alcohol. Often, a group of us would go to Hendrick's house, which was a short two-minute walk from the school gate, and drink the afternoon away while sitting under a tree. The regulars included Hendrick, Phillomon (a fellow English teacher), Benjamin (a social science teacher), Solomon (the chemistry teacher who asked me about *aluminium*), and me. Since there wasn't much in the way of patio furniture, I usually sat on a broken stool, Phillomon on top of a garbage can, Hendrick on a spare tire, Solomon on an old lawn chair, and Benjamin would share a small wooden bench with any neighbors who would stop by to chat. The marula juice would get placed in the center of our gangly circle in two separate 10-liter containers that looked like they had previously been used as fuel tanks. The screw-on gas cap was a slight giveaway. The scene looked like a Namibian version of the cartoon *King of the Hill*.

Eventually, the marula season came to an end and the social outings dwindled until they were no more. Throughout the year I became less inclined to hang out at the shabeens. Therefore, I mostly spent time with my colleagues at school events. And that's where the majority of my social life unfolded – at school.

My learner friends at Eengedjo were plentiful. Kids would stop by my house all the time. And I really mean, ALL THE TIME. One Saturday morning, a few weeks after I arrived, there was a knock on my door. Startled, I looked over at my watch. It was 6:15 a.m. There was another knock, this time louder. Since it was so early, I couldn't help but think something was wrong. When I opened the door, there stood a boy in my math class, Edward. With my eyes half open, I glared at him, waiting for his urgent message. Edward just stared back at me. Finally, I broke our prolonged silence.

"Hello, Edward."

"Good morning, sir," he said cheerfully. "How are you?"

It was much too early for weekend chit-chat, so I calmly asked him, "Edward?"

"Yes, sir?"

"Do you have a watch?"

"No, sir. I am not the owner of a watch," he said, "but I would very much like one." His suggestive manner indicated he thought I might present him with an early morning gift.

"What time is it?" I asked Edward.

"It is morning, sir," he replied confidently. This was another cultural mannerism I was beginning to take note of. Detailed information was not always easy to come by.

"Yeah, I know that, but what time is it right now?"

"I do not know, sir. I am without a watch."

"Can you take a guess?" I asked him.

Edward thought about this for a moment. "Hmm…I imagine it's almost breakfast time."

Ugh, this is going nowhere.

My attempt to subtly imply he was knocking on my door way too early had failed, so I cut right to the point.

"What is it you need, Edward?"

"Sir, will you be opening the computer room?"

"Edward, it's 6:15 in the morning," I said and showed him my watch.

He looked confused. "If you know the time, sir, why did you ask?"

He's got you there!

"Edward, I'll open the computer room, but not right now. It's too early." However, this was a matter of perspective. Just because it was too early for me did not mean it was too early for Edward. As I looked beyond him, out onto the school grounds, I could see quite a few learners were already up and about.

"Sir, what time will it open?"

"I don't know…maybe around nine o'clock."

"Very well, sir. I will return at nine." Edward turned around and walked off. I watched him go sit under a tree in front of my house.

Is he just going to wait there until nine o'clock?

I returned to my bed and unsuccessfully tried to go back to sleep. I thought about opening the computer room, but I didn't want to set a precedent of opening it so early. Instead, I went out to the living room and got on the Internet. In Omungwelume, the only way to go online was with a portable 3G Internet device. Assuming I had reception, the 3G device worked fine except the connection speed was about as sluggish as the pace of rural living. The device worked similar to a prepaid phone, but instead of buying minutes, I would buy megabytes in the form of scratch-off cards, with one Namibian dollar being equal to one megabyte (MB) of information. Therefore, if I wanted to download a song that was 4 MB, it would cost me $4 Namibian, roughly 50 cents U.S. Using the Internet could get costly, especially on a volunteer's salary. But still, it was my only connection to the outside world.

As I looked out the window, I thought about the learners. They didn't have an immediate connection to a life outside of their own. Their world existed in front of them, not in cyberspace. Remarkably, Edward sat under the tree for the next couple of hours and watched the morning whittle away. His internal clock was right on time. Edward returned to my door precisely at nine o'clock, and together we walked over to the computer room.

On weekends, the kids continued to knock on my door early in the morning. It was usually the same routine. When I opened the door, I would always wait for the kids to speak. After all, they were the ones who were looking for something. When it became apparent they weren't going to say anything, I would ask them what they needed. It wasn't until months later that another WorldTeach volunteer explained to me what was going on. His Namibian roommate told him that when a guest comes to another person's home, it is culturally appropriate to wait until the owner of the house greets the guests and invites them in. This explained the staring contests I had had with the learners when they came to my door.

The early morning questions I would get were never the urgent kind.

"Sir, can you take our picture?"

"Sir, will you borrow me a basketball?"

"Sir, do you have any magazines?"

A few weeks after Edward paid me a visit, it all came to a boil. I got a knock at 5:40 in the morning from a boy in grade 8. "Sir, will you be showing us a movie this evening?"

After that incident, I began to put a notice up on my door: **Do NOT knock if it's before 9:00 a.m.** I never considered if I was being culturally insensitive. At the time, I didn't really care. The learners had a completely different concept of boundaries. They assumed if they were awake, then I would also be awake. However, they respected my wishes once the sign was taped to the door. Still, at around 8:30 in the morning, learners would come and sit outside my house, waiting for the 9 a.m. opening.

Throughout the day, learners would pop in for one reason or another. Most commonly, I would get requests involving mp3 players or USB storage devices. The kids usually wanted me to either add music to the devices or remove a virus. On occasion, I would get homework questions which I was more than happy to help answer. Other learners would come by just to chat. They were curious about America and some of my other travels. They also loved looking around the house and were quite taken by my electronics. The learners were very impressed with my iPod and digital camera, but everyone's favorite activity was to watch the screensaver on my computer because it would show photos when activated. The learners could sit and watch it for hours. It came as no surprise the learners had a strong fascination with such luxuries. In Omungwelume, there were more donkeys than there were cars, and technology was perhaps the scarcest resource of all. In general, I didn't mind the learners visiting me at home. While at Eengedjo, I experienced enough solitude to appreciate the value of companionship. The learners became one of my social outlets, and I enjoyed their company as long as it wasn't before breakfast time.

By the middle of the second term, roughly halfway through my year-long commitment, it became evident who my closest friends were. It's not who I would have imagined to be at the nucleus of my social group. After all, they were learners.

It all began with a girl named Johanna, the same girl who had baffled me by asking for a rubber (eraser). Johanna was 14 years old. However, given her small stature, she could have easily passed for 11. Johanna had short braided hair, a common style among many of the girls, and her plump, rounded face slightly resembled that of an Oompa Loompa. She looked innocent enough, but she carried around an inquisitive expression that was both blameless and mischievous.

Towards the end of the first term, Johanna made a point of stopping by my house in the afternoons. Soon enough, more of the girls from my math class began stopping by with Johanna. Often, I think it was because they had nothing else to do. They would come by to chat and loved looking at the pictures on my computer. However, their favorite activity was scavenging around the house looking through old magazines, notebooks, and boxes that were left behind by previous volunteers. They would find random objects and ask me, "Sir, who is the owner of this?"

"Who is the owner of this crayon?"

"Who is the owner of this pencil?"

"Who is the owner of this book?"

The girls were hoping I would allow them to take some of these supplies, but I was careful about what I gave to the learners. If I just hastily gave stuff away, all the learners at Eengedjo would have been coming by to hoard the miscellaneous materials in my living room. But the girls were persistent in asking for items I didn't want, didn't need, or didn't even know were in the house. And since I was unwilling to just give things away, we eventually came to an arrangement – laundry.

People in the developed world are spoiled when it comes to doing laundry. There are fancy washing machines with different spin cycles, and dryers with different temperature settings. The biggest hassle is folding the clothes. But laundry is a bit more tedious and time consuming in rural Namibia since it is done by hand and then hung on a clothes-line to dry.

The staging area for my laundry theatrics was at the back of my house. For the first couple of months, every time I did laundry, learners would stop by to enjoy the show. The performance was pathetically comical. If I were to earn a grade for washing clothes, I would definitely have received a U. After filling the tub with water, I would add powdered detergent. Then I would throw a few items of clothing into the tub and rub the fabric against itself. I thought I was doing pretty well, although the learners' laughter made me think otherwise.

"Sir, you are not doing it right," they would tell me. "You need to make sound."

"What sound?"

Reluctantly, I allowed the learners to demonstrate. When they rubbed the fabrics together, they somehow collected soap suds, and it made a squishy sound. I tried again. No sound! It was a bit frustrating. The learners always offered their assistance, but I refused. I was determined to be self-sufficient, although I was still far from acquiring such know-how.

The girls in my math class were no less critical about my washing skills. When they asked if they could help, I declined, and they seemed mildly upset. In the Ovambo culture, it is a great honor for younger children to be able to provide a service for their elders. But I knew I would feel guilty if I were to allow them to wash my clothes. It's strange, but sometimes I think guilt may be an inherent part of the American culture of excess. In time, I discovered the other teachers who lived on school property allowed learners to wash their clothes. This ameliorated some of my guilt, and I quickly came to terms with the fact that I was awful at hand-washing clothes. Eventually, I acquiesced to the girls' pleas and allowed them to take over. Since I was kicked off washing detail, I then became designated clothes-hanger.

The girls were an immense help when it came to laundry. It would have taken me over a half hour to wash what they could get done in five minutes. After helping me with my laundry, I would show my gratitude by offering them some of the very school supplies they would inquire about. Sometimes I would share snack food with them because they always claimed to be hungry. I was actually happy with this arrangement because it saved me a lot of trouble. It even got to the point to where they would ask if I needed anything to be washed, although I think this may have been a round-about way of saying they wanted something to eat.

I got used to the girls coming around and enjoyed their company. I never would have thought that in my adult years, there would be a time when my closest friends were a group of 14-year-old girls. It may sound weird, but I kind of felt like a father figure. I had six daughters at the school, and when you are so far out of your own element like I was, it's nice to feel like you have family.

Getting help with my laundry

In truth, I spent a great deal of my time alone, even with occasional colleague outings to a shabeen and learners frequently stopping by my house. My closest friends were the other volunteers in the program, but since I didn't travel most weekends I would only get to see them about once a month. Thus, I had an ample amount of time to get to know myself. Eventually, there was fallout from my lack of companionship, and the solitude started to get to me.

Talking to myself became endemic throughout my time at Eengedjo. My mental state went from having thoughts using my inner voice to actually verbalizing the dialogue taking place in my head. Surprisingly, there is no word in English describing the act of talking to oneself. There is only the expression "thinking out loud." However, many people probably opt for the word *crazy*. I began to wonder if my social constraints were, in fact, unhinging my state of mind.

Over the years, psychiatrists have repeatedly suggested talking to yourself may actually be healthy. Research has shown that talking to yourself is a great way for people to remember things. For example, if someone loses their keys, talking out loud while looking for the keys may help the person remember where they are. People also talk to themselves to release stress, often in the form of humming or whistling. In addition, talking out loud helps us understand complex information. When verbalizing the information, hearing the language helps us remember the exact words. But none of these cases applied to me. I was not looking for anything. I was not stressed. And I was not trying to remember complex information. I was creating imaginary scenarios, both real and fictional, and talking them out. After a while, I began physically acting out some of the scenes in my house. Perhaps I **was** going crazy?

One amazing feature of the Internet is we are now allowed the convenience of self-diagnosis. Of course, this is ill-advised, but I imagine people "Google" their problems all the time. My own self-diagnosis indicated I was likely experiencing a form of disassociation brought on by social isolation. This could be completely wrong, but it sounded good. Disassociation is a type of defense mechanism that serves as a kind of psychological protection. I was engaging in these mental role plays to distract myself from my loneliness. This psychological protection blocked out the reality that I did not have a satisfying social outlet. Of course, I enjoyed visiting with the learners and spending time with my colleagues outside of work, but deep down these interactions did not equal the social fulfillment I received when spending time with the other WorldTeach volunteers.

The only bright side to this behavior was that it didn't manifest itself in social situations. I didn't forget social etiquette or ignore people in group situations. Basically, when I was with other people, I got to pretend everything was okay. But behind closed doors, the real world of seclusion became lackluster. Therefore, I returned to being

Wes Weston – covert operative, World Cup champion, intrepid explorer, and debonair ladies' man.

As time went on, my fantasies became more conspicuous, and I couldn't contain them anymore. I became starved enough for conversation that I sometimes talked to myself in front of other people. Usually, it was a situation where I would be surrounded by others, but not directly socializing with them. On a few occasions, my colleagues who sat next to me in the staff room would ask if I was talking to them. Of course, I would tell them I was and then make up some silly question off the top of my head. Yet the full extent of my nuttiness was when I would make myself laugh. All of sudden, I would start laughing and sometimes others would catch me in the act. As time went on, my fantasies became more conspicuous. My family even noticed this habit when they came to visit me. In hindsight, I think I was partially losing my mind.

My lack of a social life made me realize I wasn't cut out to serve as a volunteer longer than one year. Initially, I came into this experience with an open mind as to how long I might stay. Although I enjoyed teaching at Eengedjo, and I most definitely would have been a more effective teacher the second year, the social environment exposed my limitations. Ultimately, it's what helped me make my final decision. For several months, I wouldn't tell the learners if I was going to extend for another year. Whenever they would ask me, I would tell them I wasn't sure. But once I hit the six-month mark, I began notifying learners I would be leaving at the end of the year. Most were okay with this and didn't throw any guilt my way. They knew I was far away from home, and figured this was the cause for my upcoming exodus. I didn't see any reason to tell them otherwise.

Out of the 14 volunteers in our group, four ended up extending for another year. I knew some of the other volunteers acclimated into their communities better than I did. But overall, I believe everyone experienced challenges within their relative social environments. It's not easy when you're out there on your own. Living in the Namibian bush certainly tested my mental and emotional fortitude, but on the plus side, it provided me with the opportunity to know who I really am.

Chapter 15
Time is NOT of the Essence

Life in Namibia was slow. And I had even spent a year in Costa Rica, which is known for its laid-back, "Pura Vida" lifestyle. But living out in the rural farmlands was different. When it comes to speed, life in Omungwelume kept a slower pace than the donkeys that roamed around the village. No matter what it was – a staff meeting, school activity, or even regular classes – a sense of urgency was never part of the agenda.

As an American, I always seemed to be in a hurry compared to the slow and deliberate pace of Namibians. When I would walk to class, I would pass many of my colleagues at about three times their speed. Somewhat poking fun at me, they would comment, "Ooh, Mr. Wes. You are always in such a hurry. The learners are not going anywhere."

Actually, I just like to take a full stride when I walk.

I always kept my thoughts to myself, and I never really felt I was moving fast unless walking alongside another colleague. But by far, the learners were the ones who kept the slowest pace at Eengedjo. If there were a strong gust of wind, they probably would have started moving backwards. At the end of the year, I made a school video that was a compilation of pictures and videos, and called it *Knowledge is Strength*. One part of the video was a two-minute time lapse which showed the learners changing classes. I sped up the video so the learners looked as though they were moving incredibly fast. When I shared the video with the learners at the end of the year, they thought the time-lapse was hilarious. However, physical speed was not the only distinguishing feature when it came to timeliness.

Cultural discrepancies greatly dictate the variance in which people adhere to an internal clock. In America, it's customary for guests to arrive a little late for a party, hence the expression "fashionably late." But in Omungwelume, the perception of time transcends the boundaries of just evening soirees. Time perception is pervasive in people's social lives, and it applies to lateness, scheduling, and a considerable amount of patience.

My first exposure to rural time perception was with school events. I was surprised to find out the learners, as well as the teachers, have a strong affinity towards beauty pageants. There were two competitions held on different weekends in the school's dining hall, Miss Valentine's for the girls and Mr. Independence for the boys. Even though Valentine's is celebrated in February, our Miss Valentine's pageant was appropriately held in March. And although the country's actual Independence Day is in March, we had the Mr. Independence competition in April. Slowly, I was starting to learn nothing happens when it's supposed to happen.

The duration of these events also epitomized how Ovambos schedule time because events felt like they would last forever. During the beauty pageants, there were intermissions between wardrobe changes when groups of learners would give musical performances of *kwaito*, which is a mix of hip-hop, house music, and African beats. *Kwaito* is a lesser known music genre that emerged from Johannesburg, South Africa in the 1990s, but it's more than just music; it's also a dance. During performances, learners would hop around and shuffle their feet. These performances were nice, but they greatly prolonged the evening. From start to finish, both pageants each ran over four hours long. At Eengedjo, patience was definitely a virtue.

I didn't fully realize just how long events could last until the school had its Cultural Presentation. All the learners participated in the event, and each class presented a part of their culture and then performed a traditional dance. One at a time, each class walked into the dining hall, clapping in unison while chanting a song, and then formed a semi-circle in front of the judges. When the clapping stopped, one learner from the class would come forward to make a presentation about Ovambo culture. The learners brought forth pottery, basket weaving, and woodwork since Ovambos are known to be skilled artists. They also presented food, displaying the most common crops traditionally harvested by the Ovambo people. They had beans, squash, sorghum, and most notably millet, which is the primary crop throughout north-central Namibia and locally known as *mahangu*.[6] At the time of the Cultural Presentation, I was still learning much about the Ovambo culture. But the learners' presentations of artistry and food put much of the culture in perspective.

The presenting class stood out from the rest because those learners were dressed in accordance with Ovambo custom. The girls wore a vibrant traditional pink and red skirt, along with a white top, which was either a spaghetti strap undershirt or the white school uniform rolled up and tied together at the midriff. The boys, on the other hand, wore only a pair of shorts and no shirt. All the learners were barefoot, which coincided with their dancing. Once the spoken presentation was over, the entire class would resume clapping and chanting. Then, individually or in groups of two, learners would enter the middle of the semi-circle to dance. The traditional Ovambo dance consisted of a rhythmic stomping of the feet. The melody they

---

[6] The production of *mahangu* plays an integral role in the lives of many people in rural Namibia. Traditionally, *mahangu* is pounded with a large wooden pole until it becomes a fine white powder, and this is a process still used in many rural households. Afterwards, it's typically used in one of two ways. Most commonly, people make a stiff porridge known as *oshifima*, which is one of the most prominent staple foods throughout Namibia. The other use for *mahangu* is fermenting it to make an alcoholic drink called *oshikundu*, which is always home-brewed and then sold locally.

created was unique. Every time a foot hit the concrete, it made a pronounced sound, which created another beat alongside the clapping. The dance lasted for several minutes, and then the learners would exit the same way they entered. Although it was by far the coolest event I witnessed at Eengedjo, it was also the longest. The Cultural Presentation ran for nearly five hours, and after all 19 classes presented, it was almost 1:30 in the morning.

Staff meetings also exemplified rural time perception. Each term our school would hold two major staff meetings, and at these meetings we would discuss a variety of topics, such as upcoming events, the school budget, and policy changes from the MOE. Many teachers would show up late for these meetings, which meant they would never start on time. Then, once the meeting did get underway, it would unnecessarily drag on. The school principal, Mr. Joseph, had many admirable attributes, but the fact that he loved to hear himself speak was not one of them. He could ramble on for several minutes on a topic that could be summarized in just a few sentences. At these meetings, we would have a list of talking points go through, and the result was just about always the same. After the principal would pose an issue, we would discuss it in an open forum. In the end, few issues ever got resolved. Finally, the principal would suggest we choose a committee to look into the matter. And that's how we would move from one topic to the next topic. We would form committees.

Forming committees was something our school did best. If there was a national competition for forming committees, Eengedjo would have been tough to beat. We were committee-forming all-stars, and we formed committees for just about anything and everything: quality of school food, snack shop hours, even television use in the staffroom. At one point I was supposedly a part of three different committees. But the committees hardly ever met, and there was rarely any follow up. Ultimately, it was an efficient way of putting things off.

What surprised me most from these staff meetings was everyone's complacency with such a long, drawn-out process. My colleagues seemed to endure this lack of timeliness much better than I could. But I didn't realize just how much more tolerant Namibians were when it came to scheduling time until Eengedjo had its first parent/teacher conference.

Towards the end of the first term, the school held a meeting between the parents and teachers. Parents, relatives, and guardians of the learners were invited to attend. The meeting was held on a Saturday, and during the Friday morning staff meeting, Mr. Joseph stressed the importance of punctuality. The meeting was scheduled to begin at 9:00 a.m. and ALL TEACHERS should be in the dining hall by 8:00 a.m.

I thought that I was beginning to understand how Namibian time perception worked, so I ignored the principal's request and showed up about a half hour late. When I arrived, the only people there were the principal and a couple of the department heads. Mr. Joseph walked up to me and shook my hand. "Ooh, Mr. Wes, you're early."

Actually, I'm 30 minutes late, but I know what you mean.

I just smiled at the principal and accepted his praise. Some of the learners were organizing the seating arrangement, so I helped them move the benches as the rest of the teachers began to roll into the dining hall. By 9:00 a.m., just about all the teachers were present. The meeting was supposed to start. But there was one group still missing – the parents.

Over the next hour, parents began to enter the dining hall and get seated. I was seated in a line with the other teachers against the back wall, with the parents directly in front of us. Just after 10 o'clock, the meeting commenced. I caught a glimpse of the upcoming agony when I got a hold of the meeting's program, which listed 17 items to discuss.

I should have brought a book!

The first item on the agenda was a welcoming song by the school choir. A group of learners entered from the back of the dining hall and danced their way to the front while singing in Oshikwanyama. They faced the parents and continued to sing a beautiful tribal song. But even the song was privy to time perception. It just kept going, and after 20 minutes the principal actually had to cut them off. The choir truly set the tone for the rest of the agenda. Mr. Joseph then gave his opening remarks, which we endured for 45 minutes. At 11:30 a.m., it was on to item number three.

One by one, teachers, board members, and guest speakers strolled up to the podium and went into long dissertations in Oshikwanyama. I occupied my time by playing Sudoku on my cell phone or watching birds playfully chase each other around the dining hall rafters. From time to time, a female colleague sitting next to me would give me the meeting's cliff notes. After one woman spoke for a half hour, my colleague leaned over and said, "She was talking about the school garden." The next person spoke for only 15 minutes, which my colleague summed up by saying, "Um…she really didn't have much to say." I only wish the speakers could have been as pithy with their statements as my colleague.

Sometime around 2 o'clock my phone died, which meant I was puzzleless. My other colleagues were well-equipped for the meeting, having brought newspapers, mp3 players, even food. As the agenda crawled towards the finish line, my knees began shaking uncontrollably. I couldn't hold still. I marveled at the serene disposition of the parents. Everyone seemed impervious to restlessness. Finally, the principal approached the microphone, looked at his watch, and indicated it was time to wrap things up.

Thank God! I'm starving and need to go to the bathroom.

Mr. Joseph, however, talked, and talked, and talked. It made me wonder what he said in Oshikwanyama after he looked at his watch.

Okay parents, it's getting pretty late. So for the next hour I'll leave you with these parting words.

After the principal spoke, there was about a half hour of questions and comments from the parents. Miraculously, we arrived at item number 17 – the closing prayer. But it was too late for my prayer to be answered. It was already 5:30 in the afternoon. The meeting had gone on for over seven hours.

Every culture has idiosyncrasies with regards to time. Most of my colleagues would agree that meetings, programs, and events never started on time and would last way too long. However, they viewed this as a part of life as opposed to a great inconvenience. It would not drive them crazy in the same way it would me. But why are there such differences in the way cultures perceive the value of time? Is there a social scientific explanation behind this? The answer is yes.

Chronemics is the study of nonverbal communication in an intercultural setting. It shows how an individual or group perceives the value of time, and assesses the way in which people handle and structure their time when communicating. This past century, the cultural landscape has changed significantly across the globe due to technological advancements from the invention of the airplane to the Internet. Given the prolific spread of values and ideas, scholars and academics have begun to thoroughly scrutinize why certain cultural differences exists. In the late 1950s, Edward T. Hall was at the forefront of cultural research. Part of Hall's research focused on nonverbal communication, and he asserted that people's perception of time is embedded in their culture and often expressed through nonverbal communication. The different ways cultures value time may be exhibited in daily agendas, punctuality, speed of speech, movements, and willingness to wait. Hall explained this further by placing cultures into two different categories of time perception: monochronic and polychronic.

Many developed Western nations adhere to a monochronic time perception and fully embrace the notion that time is a resource not to be wasted. In their daily lives, people invariably schedule their ti... into precise units. They try to manage time effectively for both personal benefit and financial gain. Within a monochronic system, time is seen as linear, which means it has a starting point and an ending point. We tend to package our time neatly before shipping it off into the past. People adhere to a clock, and characteristics such as punctuality and promptness are considered good manners. Given my American social traits, Namibians thought I was always in a hurry, or they may not have understood my impatience when it came to lengthy meetings or events.

On the other end of the spectrum is the polychronic time perception. Many societies throughout the world in Latin America, Africa, Asia, and the Middle East use a polychronic system of time. In this system, much less emphasis is placed on the clock. Time is perceived as being circular, with no beginning or end, which entails there is less anxiety about the future. Instead, polychronic cultures view time as part of their relationships with other human beings. Therefore, within such cultures, people are more prone to build strong, long-lasting relationships. In addition, these cultures believe many things can be done at the same time, which means plans are not always scheduled accordingly. Many rural communities adhere to a polychronic time perception, and this time system can most aptly be described in the words of another cultural researcher named Raymond Cohen. In the book *Negotiating Across Cultures*, Professor Cohen remarks that polychronic cultures are steeped in tradition, noting that communication within these societies is not dictated by a clock, but grounded in the changing of the seasons. Time, therefore, moves according to the invariant pattern of rural and community life. While living in Omungwelume, I began to take notice of this truth.

It's important to note that time perception, especially among different cultures, is not an absolute. People view time relationships differently on the scale between monochronic and polychronic time systems. In rural Namibia, the adherence to a polychromatic system is quite evident. But how does the Ovambo culture specifically lend itself to this time perception? Some aspects of time perception were clearly visible, such as the length of school events or people's willingness to wait during long meetings. But there are subtler forms of time perception that are not easily seen on the surface.

When examining the Ovambo culture, it's important to understand the value of human relationships. Not only is the family a cornerstone of unity, but the entire village falls within this framework. Neighbors take care of each other's kids, and in many ways the community functions like an extended family. Even at school, the learners would refer to each other as being brothers or sisters, although they may not actually be blood relatives. This level of closeness exemplifies how Ovambos characterize an individual's worth. In both Ovambo and America culture, a strong emphasis is placed on the individual. However, the meaning of that emphasis is completely different. American individuality stresses what is important only to the individual, and the desires of others are seen as irrelevant. Ovambo individuality takes into account the needs of other individuals. Essentially, what is important for one person is also crucial for the group. Transportation is an example that shows this veiled, subtle attitude.

When traveling long distances, people don't often use hikes. The public transport system is comprised of old minibuses (known as *komibis*) that run to most major towns across the country. *Kombis* have no official schedule and leave only when full of passengers. Thus, people sometimes have to wait hours before leaving for their destination. Then, once the trip gets underway, there is often a number of interruptions. A trip from Oshakati to Windhoek takes about seven hours in a car, but in a *kombi* the same trip may take up to 10 hours depending on the number of unanticipated stops. On one of my trips to the capital, a woman asked the driver to stop at a market so she could pick up some fruit. The driver obliged and made the stop. Other passengers decided to get off and do some shopping as well. What should have been a three-minute stop turned into a thirty-minute delay. At first, I was surprised the needs of this one individual (the woman who wanted fruit) were being placed ahead of the needs of the group (everyone getting to the capital as soon as possible). At the time, I didn't realize those were *my* needs and *not the groups*. Culturally speaking, the needs of the group were not getting to the capital *as soon as possible*. The needs were simply just *getting to the capital*. Time was not really part of the equation. However, since Ovambos have a strong sense of individual worth, it's as though the needs of the individual become the needs of the group. A stop for one person is invariably a stop for everyone.

A polychronic time perception is also pervasive in everyday communication. I immediately noticed this with basic questions and answers. From my Western perspective, if I ask a question, I expect a certain kind of answer. The answer will be detailed, precise, and without delay, so I can make an informed decision. However, in Namibia, I found many of the answers I received to be vague and nondescript. It would also take several questions just for us to arrive at what I considered a satisfactory answer.

"How deep is the river?"

"Ooh, it's very deep."

"Like 20 meters?"

"Ooh, it's not that deep."

"How about 10 meters?"

"Less than 10 meters."

"One meter…two meters….three meters….four meters…five meters?"

Finally, we would arrive at an answer of five meters.

When soliciting information, it would often turn into a "How many fingers am I holding up?" type of game. However, the vague answers I was given were a reflection of the vagueness of my questions. In America, if you ask a vague question, you can expect a fairly detailed answer. In Namibia, if you ask a vague question –

"How much does an elephant weigh?" – you could expect an answer such as, "A lot." After a while, I learned to adjust my approach. In order to get a detailed answer, I would have to inquire with a detailed question.

Greetings is another example of how Ovambos value time through human relationships. In Oshikwanyama, simply saying "Hello" is a two-part process. Here's a sample dialogue between the school security guard, who didn't speak English, and me.

Wes: Walelepo? – *Good morning.*

Security Guard: Ehee! – *Yes!*

Wes: Nawatuu? – *Are you well?*

Security Guard: Ehee! Ovewalelepo. – *Yes, good morning.*

Wes: Ehee! – *Yes!*

Security Guard: Nawatuu? – *Are you well?*

Wes: Ehee! – *Yes!*

Given this linguistic nuance, it is not possible to say a quick hello in Oshikwanyama because the indigenous language does not lend itself to superficial greetings. The language actually caters towards people forming relationships. In order to appropriately acknowledge someone, people have to stop and speak face-to-face. If a person did not stop but kept moving, it was rather impolite.

Adjusting from my monochronic time perception to the polychronic one was a difficult acclimation. Even though some aspects of rural time perception were hard to accept, it wasn't all so bad. Over time, the pace of rural life started to sink into my subconscious. The longer I lived in Omungwelume, the more I adapted to the local pace of life. I began to walk slower. I showed up late for just about everything. I displayed more willingness to talk to people about inconsequential matters. My perception of time was changing, and I relished some of these changes.

My favorite part of the day was in the early evening when the learners were eating dinner. I would sit outside my front door and watch the world turn. The school grounds appeared undisturbed. Donkeys would casually pass by on the dirt road next to my house as if they knew exactly where they were going. The sun would set and illuminate a magenta sky with pinkish clouds, as if I were sitting right in the middle of a children's book. Time, it felt, would come to a complete stop.

The world was spinning in all the other places outside of Omungwelume – for my friends, family, and everyone I knew. But I felt so far away from the rest of the world that time ceased to exist. I knew that as soon as I left, I would be jumping right back on life's superhighway, where everything moves at the speed of light. But while I was here, I appreciated this stationary sense of being. Each day I'd watch the sunlight deliberately creep off towards the horizon to quickly brighten the rest of the world, before returning to slowly wake me up in the morning.

Chapter 16
Coming Attractions

Life in Namibia was full of thrills. I got to see a lion from just several meters away. I went skydiving over a stunning coastline. I watched the sun rise from atop some of the world's highest sand dunes. But the greatest thrill of all was when I showed the learners *Harry Potter*.

The momentous occasion took place a few weeks after I arrived at Eengedjo. There was a buzz circling around the school that I might show a movie Friday night. After getting permission from the hostel supervisor and borrowing some speakers from a colleague, I set up the movie in the dining hall once the learners finished dinner. Since my arrival, I had been asked on a daily basis about *Harry Potter*. Do I have the movie? Will I show them the movie? When could they watch it? The learners were *Happy Potter* fanatics.

Fortunately, the school had an LCD projector. It was a luxury that came in handy when providing entertainment. Although the projector was aged a bit, it did the trick. It had a standard VGA cable I could attach to my laptop and then project the image against the far wall. During our first movie screening, hundreds of learners packed into one end of the dining hall. The kids sat on benches or on the floor, and they were practically piled on top of one another. After plugging the speakers into the audio outlet of the computer, we had created a miniature movie theater. Except there was no Dolby Surround Sound, movie previews, or buttery popcorn. There was also no silence for that matter. If our movie theater had anything, it was emotion.

As soon as the lights were turned off, I started the DVD, and the initial credits appeared – Warner Bros. Pictures, copyright infringement, blah, blah, blah. Suddenly, *Harry Potter and the Prisoner of Azkaban* appeared on the screen. I was blown away by the reaction. There was a passionate outpour of joy as thunderous applause echoed throughout the large, open hall. There were whistles, screams, hollers, and high fives. People gave standing ovations and hugged their neighbors. Some stood up on the benches and cheered. I had no idea what was happening. You would have thought Namibia had just won the World Cup, or perhaps they had all won the lottery. The atmosphere was contagious with an emotional transference of energy. Even I became giddy with excitement and began laughing uncontrollably. I was completely stunned that a movie – and the *Prisoner of Azkaban* no less – could evoke such emotion. Everyone exhibited a similar drug-induced behavior, and we were all high under the spell of *Harry Potter*.

The environment was the complete opposite e of a typical movie theater. No one stayed seated, and no one kept their mouths shut. The initial ovation began to subside, but as soon as Harry Potter appeared on the screen, trying to perform a spell under his bed covers, there was another eruption of joy. For the first half hour, the learners would applaud whenever the camera showed Harry Potter. It was actually quite astounding. The movie shows Harry Potter – applause; cut to Ron and Hermione – clapping stops; back to Harry Potter – applause. There was so much cheering going on, it was almost impossible to hear the dialogue. Most learners probably had to follow the film visually. The only time everyone would hush was during an action sequence. But still, as soon as Harry Potter did something like cast a spell or evade danger, the dining hall would explode with applause. I had never seen anything quite like it. It hadn't crossed my mind that these kids didn't get to watch many movies, and most had probably never been to a movie theater. Therefore, this was a real treat for them. But the real pleasure was mine, being able to participate in this activity and show the learners a movie that induced such immeasurable happiness.

Throughout the year, I showed the learners movies on various weekends. They loved action movies like *Indian Jones, X-Men*, and the *Fantastic Four*. I also used the projector in the classroom, and the kids would get excited when I walked into class with it. In one of my non-promotional subjects called Business Information Systems, which I taught to grades 8, 9, and 10, I would show the learners episodes from the BBC series *Planet Earth*. This incredible nature documentary examines the planet's diversity, and the learners were captivated by the animals and locations. But no matter how fascinating the video, the learners remained a chatty group.

Evidently, the learners were unfamiliar with movie etiquette. Every time we watched a video in the dining hall or the classroom, the learners would talk incessantly. It's like they preferred to be active spectators as though they were watching a sporting event. They would cheer, applaud, and talk to their neighbor about all the excitement their eyes were soaking up. I would try to tell them to quiet down, but it was to no avail. Even though it's rather trivial, silence during a movie was an idiosyncrasy that hadn't seeped its way into the community. But as movies become a more prominent activity, even out in the bush, I imagine the same modern etiquette will eventually take hold. And that's what these kids wanted – modernization, economic prosperity, jobs, and opportunities. They wanted to own computers, smartphones, cars, and whittle their day away on the Internet instead of under a tree. But even if that's not what they wanted, I believe everyone at least wanted the choice. Sometimes, I would contemplate what changes might occur in their lives with the influx of modernization. This reminded me of yet another movie called *The Gods Must Be Crazy*.

One day a learner presented me with a DVD and asked if I would show the movie. The following weekend, we watched *The Gods Must Be Crazy* in the dining hall. The movie was a huge success. It was an old comedy from South Africa which was released in 1980. The movie contained slapstick comedy which resembled that of *The Three Stooges*. The learners laughed hysterically at all the ridiculous actions, no matter how cliché or predictable. Yet the most fascinating part of the movie was that it poked fun of the banal aspects of our different civilizations while personifying some genuine truths.

The movie is set in Botswana, and the storyline – though broken into three different parts – primarily follows a tribesman named Xi. The role of Xi is played by a Namibian bush farmer named N!xau,[7] who is considered one of the country's most famous actors. At any rate, the story of Xi takes place in the Kalahari Desert, where Xi and his people live harmoniously off the land. One day, a glass bottle of Coca-Cola is thrown out of an airplane and miraculously falls to earth unbroken. Xi's people find the bottle and assume it's a gift from the gods. They find many uses for it, but unlike other amenities the tribe has, there is only one bottle of Coke. Ultimately, this exposes the tribe to the notion of property, and they soon begin experiencing feelings such as jealousy, envy, anger, and resentment. Since the Coke bottle starts to bring unhappiness among the tribe, Xi decides the bottle is evil and must be destroyed. He sets out alone on a quest to rid the tribe of this Coke bottle and in doing so discovers Western civilization.

The movie presents a view of civilization through Xi's eyes. The portrayal of several characters is completely stereotypical. Xi is essentially shown as an ignorant person who lacks knowledge of the outside world. The white Westerners who enter the bush appear to

---

[7] The reason his name is spelled with an exclamation point is because this renders a click sound. It is part of the Khoekhoe language, one of many regional languages in Namibia.

be bumbling fools who are oblivious as to how one can survive without modern conveniences. At the time of its release, the movie drew some criticism for its character portrayals. However, the depiction of these characters does share some parallels with reality. Both the learners and I shared an equal interest in our different lives. The learners were relentlessly inquisitive about technological items like my digital camera and laptop, amenities I had long taken for granted. On the other hand, I had a great deal of curiosity about the learners' lives, culture, and language. I had never harvested anything in my life, nor had I prepared my own food by slaughtering an animal. Watching *The Gods Must Be Crazy* reminded me of our differences, and it made me consider how our lives are changing.

In many respects, globalization is creeping in on even some of the most isolated parts of the world. Language is one of several identifiers. Indigenous languages are being replaced by common languages such as English. According to some linguists, over half of the world's approximate 7,000 languages may disappear in the next 100 years. Many people are concerned about such outcomes, since language provides us with a unique lens through which we can view the world. I'm hopeful indigenous languages may be preserved. My concern, however, is that Oshikwanyama and other languages will not stand the test of time. It may likely be used less frequently by younger generations until one day its words will no longer be heard.

Sometimes, I couldn't help but wonder if I was partly responsible for the decline of tradition. Here I was, at the forefront of a cultural battleground. Inadvertently, I was spreading my thoughts, beliefs, customs, and even my language. The kids at Eengedjo had already been exposed to more English than their parents. With each subsequent generation, children will likely be exposed to even more English. In that case, were there ramifications of the subject I was brought here to teach? In some ways, it almost seems as though there is a direct correlation between the prominence of English in rural communities like Omungwelume and the area's economic prosperity. Simply put, residents of these areas, especially the younger generations, want nothing more than their communities to prosper. When the kids at Eengedjo finish school, they'll want to get a job to earn money. With that money, they'll buy items like cell phones, laptops, and televisions. Ultimately, English will become a larger part of their daily lives. They'll hear it on TV. They'll speak it to people from different areas who may not be Ovambo. They'll get onto the Internet and read it while surfing the web. It's quite plausible to imagine that more exposure to English will mean less use of Oshikwanyama. Is it okay then to deem an exchange between language and affluence a worthy tradeoff? There are a lot of question marks about the future, and it's hard to say if one tongue will get permanently tied.

Even though it was not visible, I believe I caught Omungwelume at an interesting transitional period. Who knows if rural areas will ultimately be able to retain cultural values while developing the economy? But if a price tag is eventually put on these values, hopefully it won't be all for naught. In the end, people should have enough foresight to preserve their values if it's not possible to maintain them. At least, that is my hope.

Chapter 17

The Goat vs. the Washing Machine

One intriguing feature of linguistics I noticed in Namibia was code-switching, which is the changing between two or more languages within a single conversation. Quite frequently, I would hear the learners alternate between English and Oshikwanyama. Even my colleagues would switch between the two languages. Someone may start telling a joke in Oshikwanyama, and then say the punch line in English. What's interesting is that it didn't sound too strange, and people maintained a natural flow when switching back and forth. But at the same time, it seemed as though the two languages were not mixing together, but rather competing against one another. Yet language is not the only endangered aspect of the Ovambo heritage.

As the world becomes more globalized, indigenous cultural traditions are being adapted, modified, or even disbanded. And this struggle is often seen as an internal strife, a tug-of-war among different generations. Especially among indigenous cultures, tradition is typically accepted as the prevailing wisdom. However, younger generations sometimes question whether certain customs are outdated, inefficient, or even senseless.

I never understood how prevalent the cultural battleground was until the wedding of Meme Louisa ("Meme" is a title for females, similar to Miss or Mrs.). She was a history teacher in her late 20s, and a few months after I arrived, she got engaged to be married. The wedding was set for August, which was a popular time for weddings because school is out of session and families are together at their homestead. Weddings are an important custom in Ovambo culture. Nowadays, depending on the families, Ovambo weddings typically follow a Christian ceremony. Early missionaries arrived in northern Namibia in the late 1800s, and today most Ovambos consider themselves Christian and many Ovambo traditions have been replaced with Christian ones. Even though some practices have changed, the Ovambo people still try to retain some elements of cultural convention. This struggle was suitably displayed when talks began as to what type of wedding gift the staff should purchase for Meme Louisa.

Each time an event took place – a wedding, the birth of a child, or the funeral of a family member – a collection of money was taken among the staff. The money was then presented to the family to offer support, a very communal gesture typical of Ovambo culture. Of course, everyone wanted to do something special for Meme Louisa. Discussion about a wedding present began during one of our morning staff meetings, after the principal asked Meme Louisa to excuse herself. Surprisingly, the process of determining a donation amount went smoothly. The teaching staff settled on an amount of $100 Namibian (roughly $13 U.S.) per person. Given that there were 22 staff members, our wedding gift budget was $2,200 Namibian. Then came the hard part. What should we get?

We began talks of a wedding gift just before the first class at 7:00 a.m. Mr. Joseph stood in front of our group and asked for suggestions. One older female colleague, Meme Helena, inquired why we were having this discussion. To her it was simple. We should get Meme Louisa a goat. Several other colleagues agreed, so Mr. Joseph asked if that would be okay with everyone else. Another colleague, Meme Emilia, who was a younger female in her mid-20s, displayed a lack of enthusiasm for the idea.

"I think we should get her a washing machine," she suggested. Some other colleagues agreed with her. Thus, we were at a stalemate.

"Okay colleagues," said Mr. Joseph. "We have two very excellent ideas. So now we can choose. Shall we get Meme Louisa a goat or a washing machine?"

By now, I had grown accustomed to lengthy discussions and debates regarding the most trivial of topics. However, as soon as the debate began between the goat and the washing machine, I knew that I was in for the long haul.

The lines of dissention were clearly marked. Interestingly enough, the staff was divided evenly. The older generation argued for upholding cultural values with a wedding gift like a goat, since traditional Ovambo gifts during celebrations consisted of a *tombe*, which is a word meaning "something that can be slaughtered." Tombe can either be cattle or sheep, but most often it's a goat. The younger generation, on the other hand, argued for a practical wedding gift, like a washing machine, which would serve the needs of a modern family. I was reminded of what Pulitzer Prize journalist Thomas Friedman referred to with the title of his book, *The Lexus and the Olive Tree*. The book simply notes two struggles which are taking place in some parts of the world today – the drive for prosperity and development, the Lexus, and the desire to retain a cultural identity, the olive tree. Our wedding gift served as the perfect metaphor.

Meme Helena was adamant. "Always, for a wedding celebration, you should get a goat."

"Ooh, Meme Helena, that is just not true," refuted Meme Emilia. "You don't see a hundred guests show up to a wedding with a hundred goats." Some colleagues snickered, while Meme Helena appeared agitated.

"We are Ovambo, so we get her a goat!" Meme Helen exclaimed.

Other colleagues began to join the debate.

"I vote for a washing machine. They are so much better than goats."

"Ooh, but it's tradition to get a goat!"

"But what is she going to do with a goat? We have enough money, so we should get her something she's going to use."

"I like the washing machine. If I were getting married, I would want a washing machine."

"Let's just get a stupid goat and be done with it."

Neither side showed much willingness to compromise. The bell rang, and teachers should have been on their way to class. However, if there was something on the floor being discussed, then that conversation would take precedence over teaching. In this case, the learners would just sit in the classrooms and wait. At times, some discussions would narrow down to a select group of people, or just two individuals, at which point I would get up and leave along with some other colleagues.

Mr. Joseph allowed the discussion to continue and seemed reticent to intervene. Soon enough, the debate got heated to the point where people switched over to speaking Oshikwanyama, even though it was school policy to speak English during meetings. This wasn't for my benefit, but because all classes were taught in English, the school tried to reinforce its use throughout the entire day, even among the staff. However, when tensions were high, people naturally preferred to debate in their native tongue. And this was by far the most riled up I had seen people get during a staff meeting.

I listened curiously to the points being made in favor of the washing machine and the goat. I didn't feel this decision ultimately concerned me, and I wanted to get to class. But based on the fervency with which the gift was being debated, I felt that if I got up and left it may look insensitive and impolite. Thus, I stayed seated and kept my mouth shut, or at least tried to. There was a brief pause in the debate and the principal turned to me. "Mr. Wes," he said.

Oh crap, I don't want to get involved in this.

"What do you think we should get Meme Louisa for her wedding gift…a goat, or a washing machine?"

I don't know how he could possibly expect me to call this coin toss. Perhaps if I had agreed to father Daniella's children, and we had decided to wed, I could speak with a bit more authority. As it turned out, I wasn't even going to the wedding. I would have liked to have gone, especially after the fireworks in this discussion, but my family was coming to visit me. As soon as the term finished, I was going to meet them in Windhoek. Thus, all I had to offer to this debate was a little comic relief.

"Colleagues," I began, and stood from my chair as was custom when addressing a group. "What we should do is incorporate both suggestions. We should get a washing machine, then kill it, and present Meme Louisa with a broken washing machine."

People chuckled at my suggestion, and I think tensions came down a few notches. After, Mr. Joseph jokingly asked the group who was in favor of my suggestion. It was quite apparent nothing would get solved then and there. Finally, the principal proposed we think about it, talk with one another, and the following week we would discuss it again before putting it to a final vote.

Presently, Ovambo traditional values are competing for their continuance, and the discussion about the wedding gift was fascinating because it embodied a true battle of cultural values. This struggle among the staff represented a generational difference, which to me indicated that, over time, this Ovambo tradition may start to diminish. As to what other traditions may fall by the wayside is just a matter of what extent indigenous cultures, such as the Ovambos, will pursue the Lexus at the expense of the olive tree.

During the course of the next week, both Meme Helena and Meme Emilia made offhanded comments to me in regards to the wedding present, perhaps trying to curry favor. It felt like an episode of *Survivor*, with the two women creating alliances to get my vote. And something was getting voted out, either the goat or the washing machine. Thankfully, Mr. Benjamin, who was the social science teacher, championed a solution. He suggested we do both. Enough money would be collected so that we could buy a goat,[8] and with the remainder, we would purchase an appliance she could use. When it was put to a vote, Mr. Benjamin's idea received overwhelming support. So it was settled. The tribe had spoken. For Meme Louisa's wedding gift, we bought her a goat and a blender.

---

[8] I was told the cost of a goat was around $800 Namibian, roughly $115 US. I don't think there was a universal price, but much would depend on the age and size of the goat. However, this is a ballpark estimate.

Chapter 18
Killing Day

For less intrepid travelers, Africa may seem like a daunting place. The entire continent exudes a splendid mystique that arouses both excitement and apprehension. People's limited knowledge about Africa ultimately led to its nickname as *The Dark Continent.* However, as famed geographer George Kimble eloquently pointed out, "The darkest thing about Africa has always been our ignorance about it."

Essentially, a lot of the news people get about Africa has a negative stigma attached to it. People hear about corruption, civil unrest, and the dire need for aid. When I was a little kid, my exposure to Africa involved TV commercials of some old white guy walking through a dilapidated neighborhood, showing images of emaciated children while asking viewers to sponsor a child. And then of course there was Toto's 1982 hit song *Africa.* Yet these were very unreliable sources of information.

When my family decided to visit me in Namibia and we began coordinating the travel logistics, the giant question mark attached to Africa became apparent. My parents had legitimate concerns about getting around the country, crossing borders, and travel safety. After going back and forth for several months about these issues, my parents decided to allow me to be their guide on our first family safari.

At the end of August, I picked up my family at the airport in Windhoek. For two weeks we traveled across the Namibian countryside. We first visited a little German settlement on the western coast called Swakopmund. From there, we traveled north, stopping to take pictures of what locals would consider extremely ordinary. We photographed donkeys, termite mounds, and traffic signs with images of elephants. As amusing as I found their photography choices, I understood their reasons. For them, Namibia was unchartered territory, and everything from the ground up was a sensory overload.

Eventually, we arrived at Etosha National Park, the country's most popular game reserve. Etosha, which means *Great White Place* because 25% of the land is comprised of a large mineral pan of salt and clay, is 8,598 sq. miles of protected land and is home to 114 mammal species, 340 bird species, 110 reptile species, 16 amphibian species, and even one species of fish. We spent nearly two days driving around the park and got to see giraffes, elephants, zebra, kudu, wildebeest, and a rhinoceros. However, the highlight was getting to see a lion from just several meters away. We watched as a pride of lions moved across an open field, making a group of zebra and wildebeest run off in the opposite direction. In true Namibian fashion, the lions were walking slowly and without a sense of urgency. One lion and her cub stopped to lie down in the middle of the field, while another lion appeared to be heading straight for our car.

When we first noticed the lion walking in our direction, she was about 100 meters away. Moments later she was 50 meters away, then she was 30 meters. Once she was only 15 meters away, we frantically rolled up our car windows. When the lion was just a few short meters from the car, she suddenly disappeared. The road on which our car was parked was on top of an embankment, slightly elevated above the field. The parks elevated roads, which pass through natural lands, have small drainage holes beneath them to relieve flooding during heavy rains. Apparently, the lion had decided to get out of the hot sun for a while.

A female lion just meters away

Upon leaving Etosha, we began a long trek east towards Botswana. We spent a few days at Chobe National Park where we saw more African wildlife such as massive hippopotamuses, giant alligators, spectacular cape buffalo, and numerous herds of elephants. We also got to see a couple of pristine sunsets right over the Zambezi River. After a few days in Botswana, we crossed the border into Zambia to visit Victoria Falls. With a width of 1,708 meters and a height of 108 meters, Victoria Falls forms the world's largest sheet of falling water. During the height of the rainy season, the flow rate surpasses that of both Niagara Falls and Iguaçu Falls, earning it the nickname *The Cloud That Thunders*.

As much as I would have loved to keep traveling with my family, time would not permit it. We all had to get back to the real world. My brother flew out of Livingstone, Zambia and I drove with my parents back to Namibia. I needed to back to Eengedjo for the start of the third term and they had to catch a flight out of Windhoek. In the end, my family had nothing but wonderful things to say about their time in Southern Africa. The trip certainly put at least a small part of the continent in perspective, and the journey may have shed a little light about what life is like on *The Dark Continent*.

Exploring foreign environments truly exposes a person's inexperience. It shows us how much we still have to learn about each other and our surroundings. While living in Namibia, I learned something new on a daily basis. On numerous occasions, my ignorance shone as bright as the stars of the southern skies. Yet I was humbled with all there was which I didn't know. I understood that no matter how long I were to live in Omungwelume, I may never fully appreciate rural living. This especially became evident on Killing Day.

I was about five minutes into my English lesson when the school principal appeared in the doorway. He knocked lightly on the open metal door to alert me to his presence.

"I'm sorry, Mr. Wes, for the intrusion, but we need your class." The learners began packing up their belongings as if they knew this announcement was coming.

"What for?" I asked the principal.

"They have to go slaughter chickens." It was a rather peculiar request at a school. When I was a kid, we were never excused from class to go *kill* anything. Normally, disturbances in my lessons would bother me since many requests were insignificant. But this was different. I think I was more excited than the learners.

"Okay, you heard the man. Let's go kill some chickens!"

One of the learners asked me, "Are you going to slaughter them, Mr. Wes?"

"Of course."

The learners got excited, and I could tell they were eager to see me wield a machete. I was kind of curious myself. I looked down at my fingers wondering how many I would have left at the end of the day.

The third term of classes had just gotten underway, and I had actually returned to Eengedjo only the day before. My parents had driven me back to Omungwelume and stayed the night at my house. Soon, they would leave for Windhoek. But first, I wanted to let them know about our class activity.

They'll want to see this!

Every other year, Eengedjo held a huge fundraising bazaar. It was a highly anticipated event which took place over a three-day weekend. A giant tent was going to be set up along the main road running through Omungwelume, and there would be music, performances, as well as a lot of food for sale. The main item we were selling: **chickens.**

Months earlier, there had been a discussion about the upcoming bazaar during a staff meeting. At the time, I knew very little about the event because planning was just in the initial phases. My friend, Hendrick, made a startling proposal. "I would like to nominate Mr. Wes as the person in charge of Killing Day," he said with a smile. Everyone laughed, including me, even though I had no idea what was so funny. But I proudly accepted the post, thinking Killing Day must surely be a joke. But as it turned out, Killing Day was real indeed.

The learners were given homework just before they returned home for the holiday. The assignment – to bring a live chicken back to school. Letters were sent home to parents and guardians informing them of this requirement, which had already been discussed and agreed upon at the teacher/parent conference. Apparently, the school didn't find this request to be asking too much. The chicken policy was taken seriously because learners who showed up to school chicken-less were promptly sent back home to collect one. Perhaps in rural Namibia, bringing a live chicken for a school fundraiser could be the Western equivalent of baking a cake.

Although the chickens would meet their demise, they would not die in vain. The proceeds from the fundraiser would go towards the acquisition of Eengedjo's first school bus. For some it may be hard to imagine a school without a school bus. But that was Eengedjo, with over 700 learners and no wheels to go round-n-round. The school bus wouldn't be used to pick up kids or take them home, but for transporting learners to participate in school events outside of Omungwelume. For years, Eengedjo had been saving its money for a bus, and finally the school was close to procuring the necessary finances. This year's goal was to raise $30,000 Namibian dollars (just over $4,000 U.S.). That would push us over the top, and Eengedjo could then pimp-out its first ride.

As school reopened for the third term, learners began showing up with chickens in hand. A make-shift chicken pen, comprised of nothing more than mesh wire, was set up by the front gate. Some of the chickens were able to escape and just roamed around the school grounds. But they didn't have long. With hundreds of chickens on school property, there was no time to dilly-dally. The bazaar was still several weeks away, but the chickens had to be slaughtered, plucked, gutted, cleaned, and then stored for the event. The rationale was that it was easier to keep a frozen chicken than a live one. Thus, as soon as classes began, Killing Day was upon us.

"Sir, who slaughters your chickens?"

I remember at the beginning of the year, I told some learners about my strange desire to slaughter a chicken. However, to them this wasn't strange but rather a fact of life. They eat in order to live. What they did find strange was that I had never killed one before, as if it were as normal as learning how to ride a bike.

A group of learners holding chickens for the school bazaar

"It's not like that," I told them. "The food in America is industrialized." The learners nodded approvingly, since the notion of not having to kill and prepare one's own food sounded nice.

Food in Namibia is also industrialized. There are supermarkets where people can buy their meat frozen and lifeless, just like in the U.S. What I don't think the kids were able to comprehend was just how non-agricultural the average American is, especially when it comes to subsistence farming. My agricultural prowess – zilch! I know next to nothing about the life of a farmer. Perhaps America has grown too fast for its own good, willing to exchange epochs of survival instincts for the artificial underpinnings of a culture that eagerly embraces PC's, reality TV, and Starbucks.

Being out in the rural countryside, slaughtering an animal was something I wanted to experience, an authentic part of village life. Thus, I yearned to kill a chicken. Besides, I thought it would be hypocritical of me to say that I'm unwilling to participate in the slaughtering and preparing of the very meat I happily consume. But I had never killed an animal before. I had never even been hunting. Perhaps I've been spoiled since I've never been in a position where I had to kill an animal for my own survival. Like most urban dwellers, I purchase my meat at a supermarket without a visual semblance to any sort of living creature. And no matter what kind of meat it is, I tend not to think about how the animal died.

When I walked back to my house, I found my parents packing the car. Unfortunately, they could only stay for one night because they had to catch a flight back to the U.S. It was a brief stay, but I was glad they were able to visit Omungwelume after making all the tourists stops. If anything, they were able to catch a glimpse of what my life here was like. I showed my parents around the school, and they even sat in on a couple of classes. Overall, my parents truly got to see different aspects of the country. Now they were in for one last treat.

After changing clothes, my parents walked with me to the chicken pen where some of the learners were gathered. In total, the class was going to slaughter and prepare about 50 chickens. But only about half of the chickens remained in the pen since several classes had already partaken in this activity. A few of the boys entered the pen and were chasing after the little guys. Once they caught one, they would pass it over the mesh wire to a classmate standing on the other side.

I immediately got in on the action and climbed into the pen. I chased the chickens around, and they eluded me at every twist and turn. In such a small pen, I thought they would be easy to corner, but they were quick. The learners were dying from laughter as I struggled to round up even just one chicken. However, I finally tracked one down, although the chicken may have intentionally given himself up, perhaps feeling sorry for me. I picked up the little fellow with my fist clasped around his abrasive legs. As he dangled upside down, he remained remarkably docile. I lifted the chicken up and peered into his beady little black eyes. I felt bad for the little guy, completely unaware I was about to guide him to the light at the end of the tunnel.

Once we had collected our quota of chickens, we marched back behind the dining hall where the rest of the class waited. The class captain, Jonas, was sitting in a chair while another learner, Elias, stood nearby with a machete in hand. One by one, the kids holding chickens would pass them to Jonas. He would give them a quick stretch and then lay them down across a blood-stained log. Elias would take hold of the chicken's small head while Jonas held the legs. Then, with one swift motion of the machete, the chicken met its demise. There was no sound or cry from the fallen chicken, just the thud of the blade hitting against wood. Elias would then toss the decapitated head into a pile of chicken heads, and Jonas would fling the remains of the deceased back behind him into a grassy field. There, the headless chicken joined other headless bodies in a whimsical dance of sorts. The bodies would flail back and forth, some jumping several feet off the ground. The expression "like a chicken with its head cut off" finally had some meaning.[9]

Jonas and Elias carried on like an assembly line. Their peers kept passing them chickens which they slaughtered in a matter of seconds. The entire scene was rather anticlimactic since it exuded a "business as usual" type of scenario. I don't know what I expected. Perhaps I thought everyone would be as excited as I was. But slaughtering and preparing chickens was nothing new to these kids, that is, until Elias turned and handed me the machete.

---

[9] In case you are wondering, the brain of a chicken stems down into its neck. When the cut is high, the nerves from the brain are still attached to the body and are reacting on the chickens' last impulse, which is the desire to escape. The body of the chicken will move around for a short time, but once it loses enough blood, there is no more activity. If the cut is made low enough, below the brain stem, there should be no reaction on the part of the chicken.

The level of chatter instantly rose among the spectators, who were now grinning with anticipation. I tried to appear confident and act like this was an everyday activity for an American oshilumbu. I grabbed the machete with a firm grip and gave it a good look. I have no idea what I was looking for, but at the time it seemed like the right thing to do. It was an old blade, perhaps a product of the 70s like me. Glancing beyond the tarnished silver, I could see Jonas directly in front of me clutching our next victim. I brought the machete down to my side and approached the chicken.

I asked Elias, "How hard should I hit it?" hoping that he could possibly give me some advice. He thought about my question for a moment, perhaps considering how to council me adequately.

"Hard enough," he responded.

"That's very insightful," I told him.

Using my thumb and index finger, I snatched hold of the little chicken's neck with my left hand. The chicken's diminutive stature made me a little uneasy about wielding the machete. These chickens were small, their God-given size, and not the hormone-induced super-chickens people might envision in the Western world. Selfishly, my primary concern wasn't that I was getting ready to end a life, but that I might mistakenly lose some valuable appendages in the process. If my aim was just a little off, I could completely sever my fingers. I started to second-guess the temerity of my decision to participate in Killing Day. I tried to put all worries aside as I hoisted the machete up above my head.

Without hesitating, I thrust the blade down upon the chicken like a guillotine. All I heard next was the thud sound against the wood. From my vantage point, I saw the body separate from the other side of the blade as Jonas tossed it back behind him. The blade was just a few inches from my fingers, which were still holding the chicken's head. I breathed a sigh of relief. I'm not sure if the learners were relieved or disappointed. Maybe they were hoping for a bit of drama.

I dropped the chicken's head in the pile of heads next to me, and before I knew it, Jonas was handing me another victim. I kind of wanted to take a short break, think about what just happened, and mentally prepare myself for the next slaughter. However, at this point, I had been thrust into the Killing Day assembly line. Still concerned about my fingers, I was even more cautious with the next chicken. The end result was a miss-hit, and the drama commenced.

It all happened so fast. Blood started spewing out of the chicken's neck, and the head remained loosely attached by several nerve endings. I remember hearing an "eww" sound from the audience. Then I heard Jonas yell, "Hit it again!"

I quickly raised the machete and brought it down once more, still with the power of a little girl. Blood continued to spray out all over me and the head remained attached.

"Again!" Jonas yelled. He was holding the body down with his hand since it was now starting to struggle. Another chop! Third time's the charm. The head finally detached from the rest of the body.

There was a sense of despair floating around the on-looking group of learners. I couldn't tell if they felt bad for me or the chicken. Of course if you're going to end a life, it should be done quickly. I now had blood stains spattered across my shirt and shorts. I certainly looked like an executioner, and a few of the learners were quick to point out that those stains would be tough to wash.

I was ready to throw in the towel, but Jonas wasn't about to let me quit. "Try again," he said. "But this time, hit it hard enough."

Perhaps that was some sound advice after all.

I grabbed hold of the next chicken, laid it down on the log, and chop! This time I hit it with more gusto, and it was a clean kill. We did it again, then again, and again. In total, I tallied up six chickens. It didn't take long before my curiosity about slaughtering a chicken had been met, and I was ready to turn it back over to the professionals.

Preparing to slaughter my first chicken

After the chickens had been slaughtered, one of the workers from the dining hall brought out a huge pot of boiling water. The bodies of the chickens – now lying motionless in the grass – were collected and tossed in the pot of hot water where they soaked for a little while to make plucking the feathers easier. Shortly thereafter, one by one, the learners grabbed the bodies of the headless chickens and began plucking away. I pulled a chicken out of the water and gingerly began plucking the feathers. Eventually, some of the learners mustered up the courage to tell me my plucking technique was too slow.

But I thought slow was a part of your culture?

Apparently, if the chicken dried, the feathers become more difficult to extract. Essentially, my plucking skills ranked right up there with clothes-washing skills. One of the kids finally started plucking out the feathers of my chicken with me until a small naked carcass was all that remained. The chickens were then thrown onto a grill and heated for several minutes. After getting heated, a small hole was cut at the back end of the chicken so it could be gutted and the insides removed.

As the gutting process began, it was almost noon. My parents were ready to hit the road because they still had a long drive back to Windhoek. We excused ourselves from the revelry and I walked with them to the car to say goodbye. Although my parents had showed little interest in slaughtering a chicken that day, they were excited to witness some of the festivities. And of course I'm sure it's every parent's dream to one day watch their child slaughter a chicken. Either way, it was a memorable way to end the vacation.

Later that afternoon, with my parents gone and the school grounds quiet, I resumed my normal evening position at the front of my house with a glass of wine and a pristine sunset. I reflected back on the day's events. I thought I might feel some repentance for taking the life of a living creature, but I didn't. So what did that say about me? Had rural living hardened me? Was I more in-tune with some inexplicable circle of life?

The slaughtering of animals for food is a natural process within Namibian village life. I feel more compunction for the animals that wind up in a giant American CAFO (Concentrated Animal Feed Operation) where they are slaughtered en masse. Strangely enough, not only did I have no regrets, but I actually felt good about helping to prepare our chickens for the school bazaar. I felt that as a self-proclaimed carnivore aficionado, I endured a rite of passage of sorts. Some people believe it's hypocritical if vegetarians occasionally indulge in eating meat or if they may be willing to eat fish. The line is certainly blurred. However, it's also a bit hypocritical for a meat-eater to say they are unwilling to kill for their bounty. In a way, I finally felt like I was worthy of eating chicken.

Yet the most intense part of Killing Day was my feeling of detachment. I felt utterly disconnected from everyone there, apart from my parents. I had no idea what was going on and was therefore the focal point of unwarranted attention. And the fact that all eyes were on me didn't make me feel special; it made me feel stupid. I was so far removed from this simple procedure of daily survival that seemed overtly natural to all the learners. Perhaps this was the way they felt when I took them into the computer room and tried to explain how a PC works? It's overwhelming. The learners may have been just as uncomfortable in my computer culture as I was in their farming culture. But together, we were learning.

Ultimately, the day made me appreciate how ill-equipped I am to survive in the wild. My survival instincts have all but evaporated, and everyone at Eengedjo would probably last much longer than I would if stranded out in the African bush. But still, I had taken my first baby steps. I had slaughtered a chicken and could check that off my bucket list. As I watched the sun slide down towards the horizon, I sat back in my chair completely content. That day, I felt a little bit more like a villager.

Eengedjo's brand new school bus

Chapter 19
Teaching to the Test

"Look, I'll be honest with you. There's probably a lot you could teach the learners, especially since you already have experience. But you need to take into consideration the big picture."

"What do you mean?" I asked.

Towards the end of orientation, just a few days before I was whisked off to Omungwelume, I met a return volunteer named Tim. He had taught English the previous year at a secondary school in north-central Namibia and decided to return for round two. I had a lot of questions for him because I was getting ready to teach the same subject to the same age group of learners.

Tim patiently answered many of my questions. We talked about some of the learners' common mistakes, as well as the discrepancy between learner-abilities within the classroom. It was a fruitful conversation, and I was curious what enlightening information he was about to impart in regards to the "big picture."

"Well," Tim continued. "English is everything when it comes to the learners' education. It gives them the most problems, and at the same time it's the most critical school subject."

Upon arriving at Eengedjo, I quickly realized the importance of English. Up until independence in 1990, the country's official language was Afrikaans. Afterwards, the government wanted to veer away from the previous oppression during Apartheid and therefore decided to make English the national language. Officials believed English would benefit the country in the global market, while serving as the linguistic glue which tied different indigenous groups together. Over time, English is supposed to become one of the first languages of many Namibians.

Given the enormous amount of emphasis the Namibian education system places on English, I felt both excited and anxious about the upcoming challenge. I was more than up to the task of being responsible for the single most important subject of a learner's education. Before the year began, I envisioned how I would cover the material, the tone I would set for the class, and the methods I would use for improving the learners' English. I planned to exceed all expectations. But suddenly, Tim burst my bubble.

"In my opinion, if you really want to help these kids, when you get to your school ask for some old examinations and study the format."

Really? This is your recommendation? Teach to the test?

I kept my surprise to myself as Tim continued, "These exams are fairly standard – the reading comprehension passages, the grammar applications, the writing assignments – so you know what to expect. And these are things the learners really need to practice."

Tim was referring to the national examinations that grade 12 learners take at the end of the year. The assessment exam is the all-important exclamation point on their secondary school education. But should the exam really be my primary focus?

I thought about what he meant by the big picture. At the time, I was having difficulty understanding such rationale. But then again, I had not yet experienced the situation.

"Is that what you spend a lot of time on…exam prep?" I asked.

"Unfortunately, yeah. I try to mix it up. But since the national exam means so much, I feel that I should allocate a fair amount of time to it."

"So then you think I should consider teaching to the test?"

"That's up to you. I'm just saying once you get there, it becomes a different story. Exam scores are so low you'll want to do anything possible to raise them. And that's what they're going to be judged on."

When I began teaching at Eengedjo, I found Tim was right in just about everything he had said. Exam scores were extremely low, to the point where I felt that drastic times call for drastic measures. Since the national exam was the single benchmark of their educational achievement, I had to take everything into consideration. I hated the fact that all the educational eggs were being placed in the basket of a single assessment exam. I was therefore faced with a conundrum about what should be done for the greater good.

Most people in the field of education would not likely favor the notion of teaching to the test. However, this practice has become the norm across many educational institutions worldwide. This is especially true when it comes to assessment exams, which resemble a necessary evil in the world of education. Just about everyone has dealt with an assessment examination at some point in their lives because they are pervasive in the schooling environment. The most notable assessment exam I took as a youth was the Scholastic Assessment Test, commonly known as the SAT. In an attempt to improve my score, I enrolled in an academy specifically designed to help people prepare for the SAT. The course wasn't intended to enhance my academic ability. It was purely designed to teach to the test. Unfortunately, when an assessment component is added to education, a constraint may get put around both teaching and learning. Importance is placed not on the substance of the material being taught, but rather on the selected material learners will be evaluated on. Regrettably, these examinations reign supreme when it comes to evaluating a person's knowledge in a particular field or subject. Not only that, but both the business and academic world put credence in these evaluations.

When it comes to teaching, on one end of the spectrum, there are instructors who examine the achievement requirements for the course and teach without consideration of an assessment exam.

Material is learned, and learners may or may not be evaluated on it. On the other extreme, there are instructors who explicitly drill learners on specific material they believe will appear on the exam. Little regard is given to the overall understanding of the material or its application. Information is memorized and then regurgitated onto the exam.

The distortion of instruction is one of the main criticisms against assessment exams. And when there are high stakes involved, teachers start to feel the pressure. In rural Namibia, opportunities are few and far between. Therefore, I felt responsible for helping the learners get ahead in any way I could. Thus, the temptation to take short-cuts, narrow the scope of instruction, and spend more time on test prep than actual language applications became irresistible. Defenders behind the strategy of teaching to the test argue its merits, which is practice and repetition are tied into performance. Athletic coaches do this by having their team practice drills in order to develop the necessary skills needed during competition. Improving one's typing ability is another example, and the singular instruction of finger arrangement is greatly emphasized. These practices aren't necessarily unethical. Some people even contend teaching material not on the actual test is rather illogical. No matter which side of the debate you're on, teaching to the test is a dilemma nearly all educators inevitably face.

When I first arrived at Eengedjo, I did my best to give the learners a well-rounded approach to learning English. I wanted the learners to study the language, not some exam. As the days progressed, my conviction towards this position began to waver. In just over six months, I had changed my tune. Truthfully, I wasn't even aware of how drastically my lessons had changed. It seemed to take place on some subconscious level, until one day, it dawned on me.

On a random morning during the second term, I became frustrated with one of my English classes. In general, it was a studious class, but for some reason they were having an off day. I had lost the learners even before I stepped into the classroom. They were either trying to sleep or had their minds elsewhere. Finally, I snapped. But instead of getting angry, I got emotional. I told the learners the most difficult part of my job is caring about their education when they exhibit a high level of indifference. And if I were to stop caring about their education, then I should really find another job. I then asked the class if they knew what it is I wanted from them.

"Work hard!"

"Pay attention!"

"Do all the homework."

They were all admirable requests, but none were correct. I told the class that after I leave at the end of the year, my one true wish was that the following year, I wanted to hear that every single one of them passed the national exam. Even if it weren't financially possible for them to attend university, they should at least give themselves the opportunity.

After class was over, I had time to cool down and organize my thoughts. I couldn't believe what I had told them. I was preaching the most important thing is for them to pass an assessment exam. The pressures of the education system, compounded by the reality of these kids' situations, had certainly gotten to me. The message I was sending to the learners was the same one they had been hearing throughout much of their schooling. The exam is all that *counts!* The message hadn't necessarily gotten lost, but the messenger may have.

As an educator, I wanted the very best for the learners. I wanted them to succeed. I wanted them to have opportunities. And in the near term, I wanted them to have the option of pursuing higher education. The question then became, how do I best prepare them to achieve these goals?

The curriculum for English set forth by the MOE was comprehensive and detailed. The MOE made it clear the learners were responsible for a thorough understanding of the English language. However, the national examinations did not illustrate the same comprehensive scope. The exams were more predictable.

The national assessment examination in Namibia consists of three different parts: reading and writing, listening, and speaking. Each part of the exam is administered separately, so it seems like three different examinations. However, the scores are tallied together for one final score. For the most part, my lessons focused on reading, writing, and listening. The speaking part was harder to study for since it was a subjective evaluation. Besides, the listening and writing portions of the exam gave learners the most trouble. As I studied the old exams, I noticed within each section there was some continuity.

The age-old axiom states that practice makes perfect. As the year progressed, I began allocating more time to completing exercises similar to those found on the exam. We completed reading comprehension passages with short-answer questions. We did writing assignments such as articles and letters. Listening activities were accompanied by worksheets where learners had to fill in the blanks or answer true/false questions. Sometimes, I presented learners with exercises from old exams, and other times, I put together my own material. For each assignment, I presented the directions in the same manner in which they would be found on the exam. In general, I blatantly began teaching to the test.

Yet, for all the exercises and activities we completed, the results did not reflect the hard work the learners put forth. At the end of each term, when the learners would take their English exam, which emulated those of national exams, the final results were devastating. Something was missing.

Eventually, it became clear that nobody had ever taught the learners how to prepare for an assessment exam. The learners were unaware of some of the basic fundamentals of exam prep. For starters, they had a tough time following directions. This would cause them to fill out information incorrectly or even write about the wrong topic. Therefore, I would make the learners do numerous exercises where the only objective was following directions. Time management was another exam prep technique we worked on. Unfortunately, most learners didn't own a watch. Even more unfortunate, there were no clocks in the classroom. The person moderating the exam would write the time on the blackboard in 15-minute intervals. After the first exam, I received many papers with unfinished writing assignments. Hence, we practiced timed writing assignments, and I tried to discipline them to be vigilant of the clock. Finally, even simple processes like making an educated guess were overlooked. Learners were prone to just leaving questions blank, even if it were a section of true/false questions. We then discussed techniques like process of elimination, or just making the best guess because something is better than nothing. Preparing for an exam is an important part of getting ready to take the exam. But the fact remained that, as time went on, I allocated more time for teaching to the test. So was this really helping the learners? Was I doing them a disservice, or was I just being realistic?

All in all, I had mixed emotions about whether or not I was making the right decision. In truth, the results from my little experiment were inconclusive. Throughout the year, the exam results from my English classes showed overall improvement, although I wouldn't necessarily equate this success to the test material I was teaching. Perhaps the results hinged more on the test taking applications we practiced. But test scores slowly got better, and at the time that was the only measure of success.

Even with me catering the lessons to the exam and despite the learners' gradual improvement, the final test results were still well below expectations. I taught two grade 11 English classes, for a total of 82 learners. The first term of the school year finished in April, and after the end-of-term examinations, only three learners had met the scoring requirements in English and point requirements in the remaining subjects to earn a *Pass* note on their reports. The rest of the reports read *Fail*. When the results were in after the second term's August exams, there were nine learners with a *Pass* notification. And after the third term exams in December, there were 11 learners who had a *Pass*. These results are somewhat indicative of the overall education system in Namibia. There has been improvement, but the end results are not nearly satisfactory enough.

Chapter 20
Run for Your Lives

At the end of the second term, Eengedjo hosted the region's annual Prize Giving Ceremony, which honors selected teachers and faculty for their hard work from the previous year. School principals, educational administrators, and notable attendees poured in from across the region. Personally, I thought this was a colossal waste of a Friday. All classes for the day were cancelled. Some learners helped prepare the dining hall for our guests, but most just loitered around the school grounds. The only learners who got any value out of this day were grades 10 and 12 learners because they had been invited to attend the ceremony. The idea was that they might gain some insight and motivation as they headed into the examination period. However, I'm not sure this was the case.

Supposedly, the ceremony's first speaker was giving us the "opening statement of inspiration." His message was directed to the learners who were in the audience that day. By now, I would instinctively tune out long presentations and would pay a minimal amount of attention at these functions.

"Adolf Hitler was one of the world's greatest motivators!"

WHAT DID HE JUST SAY?

This gentleman immediately caught my full attention.

"Hitler motivated the German people to take over Europe." The man paused to let this gem of information sink in. "That, my friends, was a difficult task."

Astonished, I glanced around at the 400 plus other people in attendance to gauge their reaction. However, everyone maintained a straight-faced look. I understood the analogy about working hard to achieve your goals, but apparently our speaker wasn't going to take into consideration how psychotic those goals may be. You would think he could have gone with a more benevolent motivator, like Gandhi.

The man continued with a brief history lesson of Nazi ambitions during World War II, while I kept wondering where they found this gentleman whose name and occupation I do not recall. The speaker was an older man with a speckled beard of black and white hairs. He wore a black suit and looked out over the crowd through dark-rimmed glasses. He had a distinguished appearance, much like a politician. And he certainly rambled on nonsensically like some politicians are known to do.

The lesson on Hitler didn't last long, and the speaker abruptly shifted his train of thought like the inexplicable transition of a dream. I continued to follow the man's speech, and he suddenly began talking about Paris, where an American educator and philosopher named Gates was standing on some street corner. I wasn't sure which iconic figure he was talking about until he said the person's full name.

"Bill Gates, one of the world's richest men, was a very heavy smoker," he said. "He smoked, and smoked, and smoked, and smoked." The speaker made a puffing motion with his two fingers to drive the point home.

Well, this should be interesting.

"One day, while in Paris, Bill Gates finished his cigarette. It was raining heavily outside. Then Bill Gates walked a few blocks to a nearby store. And he did not have an umbrella!" The enigmatic speaker elevated his voice. "When Bill Gates arrived at the store…" There was a brief pause. "…at that very moment…" Another pause. "…right then and there…" The man took a deep deliberate breath.

"Bill Gates decided NOT to smoke. Since that day he gave up smoking for the rest of his life."

What a load of crap!

The Bill Gates parable was utterly ridiculous, and I couldn't pinpoint its relevancy. To this day, I'm still trying to unravel that message. Later on, I talked with some of my colleagues who also shared my befuddlement. How were these stories supposed to inspire the learners? As the gentlemen began to wrap up his speech, he left everyone with this last anecdote.

"Every morning in Africa, a gazelle wakes up. It knows it must run faster than the fastest lion, or it will be killed. Every morning a lion wakes up. It knows it must outrun the slowest gazelle, or it will starve to death. It doesn't matter whether you are a lion or a gazelle. When the sun rises, you'd better be running."

It was an insightful proverb, and I'm pretty sure he didn't come up with it on his own, unlike the tantalizing Bill Gates narrative. At least this message was clear – push yourself each and every day in order to survive. However, this last little parable goes even deeper than that. Unfortunately, much as with the lion and the gazelle, survival is not guaranteed. In many ways, the odds of success are stacked greatly against these kids. And that's a serious issue which needs to be addressed. Because if people know their chances of survival are minimal, how do we encourage them to keep running?

"**Mr.** Wes, can you please borrow me $2?" asked a boy in grade 12. The boy was standing among a group of friends outside the staffroom. It was a brazen request, yet one I had heard on numerous occasions. But if they asked me like this, I would always correct them because – let's face it – education should be free.

"You mean *lend*," I told the boy. "*Borrow* means to take something. *Lend* means to give something. So what should you ask me?"

"Mr. Wes, can you lend me $2?" the boy appropriately corrected himself.

I didn't know if this lend/borrow exercise would actually stick, but it was a common mistake that constantly needed to be addressed.

"Now you realize," I continued, "that in either case, the intention is that you're going to pay me back the $2."

"Ooh, sir," the boy exclaimed. "But you are very rich." The other boys laughed at their friend's protest.

"That doesn't matter. If you ask me to lend you $2, then it means you plan to pay me back. Now do you want to pay me back?"

"Of course not," the boy said with a smile.

"Okay. Then what should you ask me?"

The boy thought for a moment. He eyed me skeptically as if he thought I may have been trying to trick him. Finally, the boy asked me, "Sir, can you give me $2?"

Now we're getting somewhere.

"No," I told him, and everyone laughed.

I had a longstanding precedent never to give learners money. There were enough panhandlers outside the gates of Eengedjo. Whenever I left the school grounds – whether walking around Omungwelume, Oshakati, or some other rural community – I would frequently get asked for money. What I found most peculiar was that the standard for panhandling seemed to be set at $2. Nobody ever asked for $1, $3, or $4. For some reason, two was the magic number. But regardless of this idiosyncrasy, the request was a microcosm of a much larger issue. People weren't asking me for money because I looked like a nice guy. They were asking me because I was a foreigner. People were ingrained with the perception that I was extremely rich and they were extremely poor. In some cases, this wasn't far from the truth.

On the surface, Namibia seems like a robust African economy in the upper-middle income group. According to World Bank estimates, Namibia has a per capita income of $6,826 U.S. This is a positive sign, right? But that really depends on whom you're asking because Namibia is near the top of the world's list when it comes to wealth inequality.

The Gini coefficient is one of the most common methods used by governments and international organizations to determine wealth inequality. It is a measure developed by Italian statistician and sociologist Corrado Gini. The Gini coefficient measures inequality among a population between values of distribution, such as levels of income. A Gini coefficient of zero would express perfect equality since all values would be the same. Conversely, a Gini coefficient of one expresses maximum inequality. The Gini coefficient is essentially a living value because it is constantly changing depending on a country's condition.

Over the years, Namibia has been widely regarded as the most unequal country in the world. The country has maintained an extremely high Gini coefficient when it comes to both income and wealth disparity. According to the CIA World Factbook, based on information taken in 2003, Namibia had a Gini coefficient of 0.71, the highest in the world. However, a household estimate done by Namibia's Planning Commission cited the country as having a Gini coefficient on the decline. Their analysis, according to the National Household Income and Expenditure, found the country to have a Gini coefficient of 0.61 in 2003/2004. These measures can be compared to many developed nations in the Western world, which typically maintain a coefficient between 0.25 and 0.4. Although the figures offered by the CIA and Namibia's in-house commission are quite different, the overall picture remains the same. In Namibia, there is a vast discrepancy between the "haves" and the "have nots."

In reality, Namibia is not the land of opportunity. Jobs, especially in rural areas, are few and far between. Unemployment across the country is widespread. According to a survey conducted in 2008 by Namibia's Ministry of Labor and Social Welfare, the unemployment rate is a staggering 51.2%, up from 33.8% in 2004.

Some local economists disagree with these measures and claim the real unemployment rate is around 28%. Regardless of what the rate truly is, the one statistic people agree upon is that the unemployment rate is on the rise. And this is a frightful reality for younger generations.

Presently, roughly one-third of Namibia's population is in school. Like so many other African countries, Namibia is dominated by a young demographic, and these learners will be looking for jobs when they finish their studies. Yet rising unemployment indicates these kids are joining the workforce at a much faster rate than jobs are being created. So how can teachers motivate learners with this grim reality? Even if they are able to get a solid education, what good does it do when there are no jobs to be had?

One afternoon, I remember talking to a boy named Edward who was a learner in my 11D English class. He had a strong passion for music and would perform at some of the school's events. One day he asked me if I would download some tracks of electronic beats for him because he planned to write lyrics to go along with the beats. Days later, he stopped by my house to pick up the CD I had burned for him. We listened to the music, and I watched as Edward moved to the beats and started to freestyle. His enthusiasm for music was striking. After listening to the tracks, our conversation somehow turned towards his future. I inquired if he wanted to go to university.

"Ooh, sir. You don't understand," he told me. "I cannot go to college. I'm very poor." Edward didn't seem disheartened by this, as though he were searching for sympathy. He stated it more as matter-of-fact, something he had accepted a long time ago.

"Can't you try to get a loan?"

Edward gave me an exasperated smile. I was over 10 years his senior, yet he looked at me as if he were wise beyond my years. Perhaps I was being naïve and lacked the ability to understand and accept the hardships of others.

"Sir, you know we have nothing. There are few jobs, and we are all poor."

Suddenly, I found myself at a loss for words. This was the first time I had felt a bit uncomfortable during a conversation with a learner. As I sat there with my laptop computer and fancy Lays potato chips, I felt as though I were in no position to lecture Edward on the value of hard work. Although I had worked to get to where I was in my life and had even covered my own expenses as a volunteer, I cannot claim to know what it's like to be poor. I didn't grow up poor, and my family afforded me a lot of opportunities. Therefore, I didn't feel justified reiterating to Edward the same rhetoric I grew up on – *You can do anything if you put your mind to it.*

"So, what do you see yourself doing in the future?" I asked.

"Music," Edward told me in all seriousness. "I need to focus on my music. It's my best chance."

This was something I had discovered among several learners who displayed a similar passion for music. In reality, the odds were against them. But in their minds they had a better chance succeeding as a musician than going to university. Edward thought he was more likely to become Namibia's next Kwaito superstar than become some corporate executive.

Occasionally, when standing in front of my classes, I would catch myself spouting some impromptu motivational speech trying to rally the learners around the importance of education. But I felt as though I had to walk a fine line between optimism and reality. After all, I didn't want to instill these kids with a sense of false hope. I knew the statistics. I lived in their environment, and I knew what it was like outside the school gates. Afterwards, I would sometimes feel guilty. It's as if I was trying to convince these kids there was a pot of gold at the end of the rainbow, even though I know a rainbow has no "end." In this environment, a person is not going to find gold, they have to make it. I've never actually had to experience this reality for myself. Yet here I was trying to inspire the learners to make something out of nothing, a message much easier said than done.

The truth of the matter is that the learners I taught at Eengedjo were faced with a myriad of obstacles extraneous to education which I never had to deal with. Health concerns, such as HIV/AIDS, are prevalent across rural areas. Disease not only affects the learners, but also their families. In many cases, young children become heads of the household and are forced to take on additional responsibilities. Ultimately, this may cause them to abandon their schooling altogether. Teenage pregnancy is another social concern and is rampant due to a lack of sex education. The year I was teaching, three girls became pregnant, and all three left school not to return. Many of today's youth also suffer from a lack of proper role models. Some children have lost both their parents and are cared for by other guardians, while others have only a single mother or father whom they may or may not have much contact with. Ultimately, many kids go about their lives without a solid foundation of support. On two different occasions, a learner commented to me that I was more like a father to them than their real one. It was a moving sentiment, and it helped me understand a bit more about the learners' difficulties. If these learners were to drop out of school, there was likely no family safety net, nobody to convince them to continue with their studies. I was amazed at the kids who exhibited a level of dedication and self-discipline I couldn't even begin to fathom when I was their age. They were at school because they wanted to be there, and they had the foresight to realize it was the best place to help them get somewhere in life.

When the sun rises, everyone needs to be running. And I guess part of my job was trying to help the learners keep pace. Instead of pushing them to take strides towards university, I first had to push them to reach the finish line of secondary school. But as long as everyone is willing to run, so to speak, then that's a positive sign. People want to survive; they want a better life. But still, where were we leading these kids? Were we steering them towards more job prospects? At times, it seemed as though no one knew. And when learners are unaware of the direction in which they should be running, few people will get to where they need to go.

A group of grade 12 girls preparing for the national exam

Chapter 21
The Apology

Lysias was the most reserved learner in my ninth grade math class. His mouth never opened except for the occasional laugh. He was also the biggest kid in the class. Never mind that Lysias was several years older than his peers. Even at 18 years old, he was still quite large for his age. Most learners at Eengedjo were short and lanky, the possible results of stunted growth due to sub-par nutrition. But Lysias was different. He was the elephant in the room, and he had the ears to match. They looked like two massive satellite dishes sticking out from both sides of his head. Lysias also completed the stereotypical view often associated with size and power. He was not the smartest elephant in the herd.

The reason Lysias was older than the other learners was because he had failed twice and had to repeat grades, once in lower primary and again in upper primary. Since he could not continue repeating in those school phases, he was moved along in the system. Each year, Lysias got a little further behind. And the further a student gets behind, the harder it becomes for them to catch up. Ultimately, their interest in school begins to wane.

This was the first time I had ever taught math as a school subject. Per the curriculum, the learners studied a mix of algebra and geometry. It took me a couple of months to find a rhythm, but once I got into my groove the learners knew what to expect. In a typical class, I would explain the material, give several examples, and then have them do some problems on their own while I walk around and check their work. Lysias was the first stop on my rounds, and I would spend several minutes helping him get started on the exercises. He had difficulty understanding most mathematical concepts we discussed, and it took a little longer for his light bulb to turn on.

Lysias was never eager to participate in class, possibly fearful of derision from his younger classmates. Therefore, I tried to work with him outside of the classroom. Whenever I assigned homework, most learners had no qualms about stopping by my house to ask for help. As the year rolled on, Lysias became more comfortable around me, and, on rare occasions, he would come by my house to get help with his homework. I always encouraged him to ask for help and would set times aside for us to work together. Unfortunately, whenever I tried to schedule a tutoring session with him, he never showed up.

The year I began teaching at Eengedjo, 2010, the MOE changed its promotional requirements among junior secondary students to incorporate math, along with English, as a subject learners must earn an E grade or better in order to be promoted. The fallout from this change was the potential jump in the repetition rate since there may be learners who pass English but fail math. However, the education system was in need of such changes. Overall, the learners were lagging in their mathematical skills and lacked confidence with some basic operations. Therefore, this was a change I fully endorsed. The bar needed to be raised, and the learners should be expected to perform to a higher standard.

Unlike learners in senior secondary, learners in junior secondary receive continuous assessment marks, which means the work they complete throughout the year – homework, quizzes, and exams – is figured into their final mark. As of 2010, since an E grade was required in order to pass math, learners had to earn 40% or better. By and large, everyone in my math class performed exceedingly well. Everyone…except Lysias.

After the first term, Lysias' grade was 32%. His second term grade improved, but only slightly. He scored 36%. This put more pressure on him during the third term because if he didn't score high enough, he wouldn't be able to push his average up to the minimum 40%. I tried to get tougher with Lysias and encouraged him to get additional help. But perhaps I didn't get tough enough.

Foresight and intuition. These are a couple of characteristics all great teachers should embody. With a keen foresight, teachers are able to anticipate the educational needs of their learners. It then helps teachers aptly determine how learners should be dealt with in the present. In order to identify learners whose educational needs require extra attention, teachers should have a strong intuition. With it teachers can properly guide learners in the right direction. However, actions are always easier to imagine than execute. But still, the fact of the matter is that the learners' success in the classroom is directly linked to how they are taught. Therefore, in a sense, if they fail, we fail.

In 2001, the United States passed an act called No Child Left Behind (NCLB). The congressional act embodied a government aid program for disadvantaged school learners. Standards and measured goals were established, and the act required academic assessments to be administered to all students, which would determine federal funding for education. The NCBL act is an example of good intentions with unintended consequences. Teachers were accused of narrowing the scope of their instruction and teaching children skills they believed would boost test scores. Many people believed having one test to determine educational quality was ridiculous. The assessment test was also criticized for cultural biases. Schools that were improving, but still did not perform to the established level of expectations, were labeled as failing. The major shortcoming of NCLB was that it was implemented at the wrong level. No government, ministry of education, school board, or principal can ultimately decide whether or not a child gets left behind. That is solely left in the hands of the teachers. Essentially, education can be encouraged from the top-down, but it can only be enhanced from the bottom-up.

When it comes to education, the value of teachers is sometimes misunderstood. Schools are only as good as their students perform, and student performance is a reflection of the teachers. Surely resources like textbooks and equipment help complement the learning environment. But as any business leader would confess about their company, its greatest resource is its people. The same can be said of schools. Successful learners are products of effective schools. And effective schools are products of effective teaching. So what is effective teaching a product of?

In 2009, the Bill and Melinda Gates Foundation set out to evaluate effective teaching in schools. The three-year project was called the Measures of Effective Teaching (MET). The goal of the MET project was to examine measures of effective teaching to adequately help teachers understand the skills that make them successful as educators and develop skills that promote great teaching. Research has shown the impact of the teacher matters most in a school, more than class size, technology, and school funding. This impact becomes even more evident at schools like Eengedjo which have large classes, little technology, and minimal funding. The teachers are not only the school's greatest resource but one of the school's ONLY resources. Therefore, if a teacher gives up on a learner, that kid has lost just about every educational advantage afforded to them.

Personally, I discovered the hardest part of teaching at Eengedjo was caring. If the learners didn't care about their education, it made it harder for me to care. I would love to say all the learners worked tirelessly, but that just wasn't the case. Some learners were very diligent in their studies, entertaining dreams of traveling abroad and attending a foreign university. Other learners seemed more fatalistic, resigned to a life of farming, not because that's what they wanted but because they felt they had no choice in the matter. Therefore, the concept of work ethic sometimes became muddled. Trying to convince learners not to give up was a job in and of itself. In the end, my teaching experience was full of highs and lows. At times the learners inspired me, and at other times they disappointed. But it's only fair to say I was also far from perfect and would even disappoint myself.

Teachers are human, and human beings are fallible. An unforeseen fault of mine was the acclimation into Namibian life. Perhaps I acclimated too nicely. Not only did I slow down my pace of life, I became complacent with the standard of education. I lowered my expectations of the learners. I started to accept the fact that many of them would not graduate from secondary school. And this level of complacency is troubling because it may accompany a disregard for a learner's educational needs. But if learners are allowed to give up, should teachers also be allowed to throw in the towel? When it came to Lysias, my intuition was correct all along. However, I lacked the foresight to know then what I know now. I knew Lysias needed a great deal of help, but throughout the year, I allowed him to turn in work that was below average. I sat by idly as he played in the computer room in the afternoons. Basically, I let my emotions get the best of me as I watched Lysias slip through the cracks. That being said, I cannot honestly say that I have never left a child behind. I left Lysias behind.

As the third term got underway, Lysias' math scores remained stagnant. I tried to come up with a schedule to work with him every Tuesday and Thursday afternoon, but Lysias wouldn't adhere to a schedule. Occasionally, I would track him down on the school property, and together we would work on his math homework. I tried to show him tough love because I wanted him to be responsible. But I hated the fact that I had to search him out, and I think he could sense my level of frustration. As a result, he became more reluctant to accept my help.

Towards the end of the semester, I calculated that in order to pass math, Lysias had to score at least a 62% on his final exam, a decent grade by Namibian standards. By Lysias' standards, this score would have been a phenomenal feat, like pulling off a hat-trick in a soccer match or pitching a no-hitter in baseball. It's an unlikely occurrence but still possible. Yet, unlike these sports, there was no opponent deterring him from achieving success. In the end, Lysias was competing against himself.

A few weeks before the exam, I caught Lysias playing in the computer room when I had asked him earlier that day to study with me. Like an angry parent, I walked over and turned off his game of *Teenage Mutant Ninja Turtles*. There was no protest on his part. Lysias just sat there with a slight smile of embarrassment. He tried to sink down in the chair, but his large frame offered no such escape. I didn't yell at him but rather pleaded with him. I told him all I wanted was two days a week for about an hour. When I asked him if he could do that, he nodded his head without looking at me. Then I asked if we could work on some math that day. He agreed and said he would go get his notebook. I thought about staying with Lysias to make sure he wouldn't elude me again. However, I returned to my house and waited. I wanted Lysias to show me he cared. Lysias never showed.

After that day, I never said anything to Lysias about studying math outside of class. I was fed up with the situation. If he didn't care, then I didn't care. The exam was coming up, and Lysias didn't seem too worried about his grade. As far as I was concerned, he was on his own.

On the day of reckoning, I watched from the staff room as learners finished the exam. Lysias was the last learner to leave the room. Afterwards, the teacher who moderated the exam brought me a stack of papers, and I began marking them immediately. Overall, the class performed extremely well, and I was very pleased with their performance. Even Lysias improved significantly. He scored a 48% on the exam, which was a dramatic improvement from his first two exams. But when averaging his score for the year, his final mark came out to 37%, just a few points shy of the minimum passing requirement of an *E* grade. If it had been one year earlier, Lysias' score would have been satisfactory. But according to the new math requirements, Lysias would not be promoted to the 10th grade, no matter how he performed in his other classes. Although it seemed unfortunate, I believe Namibia should keep raising the educational bar, even if it gets raised slowly. Sure the country has an obligation to not leave kids behind, but it also has an obligation to help kids get ahead.

At the time, I was able to keep Lysias' failure out of my mind. Since English was the most troubling course for Eengedjo learners, I assumed Lysias would not pass English either. Earlier in the term, I had asked his English teacher about his performance in her class. She just sighed and said that he wasn't doing well. But when I began compiling the reports for all the teachers, I was surprised to see every learner in both grade nine classes passed English. My first thought was that there was some sort of foul play. The English teacher was just pushing the learners along. But with the new math requirement, there was an additional check and balance. In the other ninth grade math class, six learners had failed. In my class, there was only Lysias. Thus, there were at least seven learners who wouldn't receive a free ride to grade 10.

When I discovered Lysias would not pass because of his math grade, I also discovered some guilt. Lysias was the first learner I had ever been responsible for holding back. I couldn't escape the fact that if I had not given up on Lysias, if I had encouraged him to study math and continued working with him up until the exam, he could have earned a passing grade. Throughout the year, he showed improvement. He just lacked motivation. But what he may have lacked even more was support. I tried to tell myself it wasn't my fault and that I had done everything in my power. But it wasn't true. I couldn't just completely absolve myself of responsibility. Lysias' grade was my grade.

After the examinations were finished, the learners left Eengedjo for a few days while the teachers recorded the final results and the school reports were generated. On the final day of the school year, the kids returned to collect their reports. After that, the learners and school staff were free to leave. The year was officially over. It was my last day at a school that had been my home for a year.

Earlier that morning, everyone had gathered in the courtyard, and the principal gave an extensive speech about hard work and dedication. Suddenly, and without warning, he turned the spotlight on me. The principal thanked me for my service and the work I had done at Eengedjo, which was followed by gracious applause from everyone. It was nowhere close to *Harry Potter* applause, but it was touching nonetheless. Finally, the principal asked me if I would like to say a few words.

Impromptu speeches are not my forte, but I stepped forward and spoke from the heart. I thanked the learners for a wonderful year and the staff for their support. I reminded them of the importance of education. School was their job, and it should be their number one priority. Whether the learners believed it or not, I said the staff and all the teachers, including myself, wanted nothing more than for them to be successful. And success doesn't have to be defined by a job title, credentials, or the money in your pocket. Success will be different for each one of them, as long as they find something that makes them happy. I gestured towards the teachers, and told the learners that their success is our success and their failure is also our failure. Perhaps it was my backhanded way of trying to make the teachers feel accountable. Little did I know that hours later I would be eating my own words.

My talk to the learners was the final exclamation point on my time at Eengedjo. Afterwards, saying my goodbyes was all that was left. Once the reports were handed out, the learners slowly began to vacate the school premises. They were going home for the holiday and would return a month later to start a brand new school year, one without Mr. Wes.

Not quite ready to depart, I returned to my house to finish packing my belongings. In the meantime, learners stopped by to say farewell. Goodbyes are not my strong suit, and I've never been good at parting ways. I felt conflicted about leaving Eengedjo. I was ready to move on to the next chapter of my life, but I wasn't ready for these kids to no longer be a part of my story. Visiting Omungwelume is not like taking a weekend trip. It's far off the beaten path. As much as I told myself I would come back, deep down I knew that I was probably saying goodbye forever and I would likely never see many of these kids again.

Just before noon, there was a knock on my door. I opened the door, and there stood Lysias. I was actually a bit surprised to see him. We had not spoken much since I had turned off his video game weeks before. By now, he had received his report and knew that he would remain in the ninth grade. I wondered if he had come to talk about his score, but he mentioned nothing of it. He said he wanted to say goodbye and thanked me for being his teacher. I was at a loss for words. I would never have expected this from such an introvert. I told Lysias that I was happy to be his teacher, and I hoped he would keep working hard at school. He had improved much throughout the year, and that was the objective…to keep improving.

Our meeting didn't last long. In the end, we shook hands in typical Ovambo fashion until I pulled Lysias in for a one-handed man hug. He smiled and laughed before turning to leave. I stood in the doorway and watched as he slowly walked away. He then gave one last turn and waved goodbye before disappearing through the school gate.

After Lysias left, I felt a bit empty inside. Only then did I realize my folly. I didn't do my job to the best of my ability, and the repercussions for that can be great. I wanted to apologize to Lysias. I wanted to tell him that I should not have given up on him. I wanted to let him know that he doesn't bear the sole burden of that grade. However, I let that chance pass me by. But perhaps it's not too late to make amends.

Lysias, wherever you are out there, I want you to know that you didn't fail math. We both did.

Chapter 22
Enda Po Nawa!

Leaving Eengedjo was completely surreal. Everything happened so fast. My colleague, Hendrick, was going to drive me to Oshakati where I would catch a kombi (mini bus) to Windhoek. I loaded my backpack and a small suitcase into the trunk of the car, and as I climbed into the passenger's seat I was reminded of when I first arrived at the school. I could vividly remember driving onto the school grounds, the learners eyeing me with an intense curiosity. Now those looks of curiosity were replaced with smiles, and the learners waved to me mirthfully as they flooded out of the front gate. The car slowly rolled off the school property, and we drove along a dirt road, passing a parade of learners. Figuring I would leave the kids with one last laugh, I yelled, "Enda po nawa!" out of the open window as we drove by. It was only fitting that I tell them *goodbye* in Oshikwanyama. With that, the 2010 school year was officially over.

Interestingly enough, I felt that I was leaving home instead of going home. I had lived such an itinerant life over the past decade I felt detached from any one location. Perhaps the idea of "home" had lost part of its meaning. For some reason, only when leaving a place would I appreciate the sense of having a home. In Namibia, Omungwelume was my home, and the learners were my surrogate family. Even though I was ready to leave, I was going to miss my life here.

When we reached the paved road, we turned left towards Oshakati, and I tried to visually soak up as much of Omungwelume as possible. We drove by a shabeen called Namibia United where I had a few late nights with colleagues. We passed another shabeen named the Mykonos Bar where I watched some of the World Cup matches on TV. Then there was the barbershop where I got my haircut on several occasions. There was the Tukwafa mini-market where I occasionally went shopping for snacks if I didn't feel like "hiking" into Oshakati. I had a year full of long-lasting memories in this village which we quickly drove through in a matter of seconds.

We cruised down the road I would take into town at least once a week. By now, I had acquired a deeper knowledge of the environment I had been living in. I was familiar with just about every pothole on the road, every tree that stood out in the field, and every village that hid behind a thicket of brush. I knew when the land would wake up in the morning and what time it would go to bed at night. I knew a great deal about my surroundings, but what I didn't know was if I would ever set eyes on it again.

As luck would have it, when we arrived in Oshakati, I caught a kombi just as it was leaving the parking lot. My luggage was heaved onto a trailer in the back, and I climbed into the front seat. Before I knew it, we had left Oshakati. During the long ride to the capital, I couldn't help but reflect on the past year. As slow as the time would tick away, now it felt like it had flown by. The entire year seemed almost dream-like. In a way, it's as if I were a time traveler getting ready to jump back into the fast-paced hustle of the modern world. When I first came to Namibia, I was a little scared. Inexplicably, I felt a similar apprehension now that I was getting ready to leave.

Before moving to Namibia, I considered everything I was giving up. What came to mind were comforts not essential to survival, such as hot showers. Other amenities, like Internet, washing machines, television, and air-conditioning, were even more trivial. Still, I knew when I arrived at my placement and the year got underway, I was going to miss many of these conveniences. In the end, some were easier to go without than others. But I got by okay. And now that I was leaving, I wasn't thinking about the superficial amenities I would welcome back into my life. Instead, I thought about everything I was once again giving up. There was so much I was going to miss about life in this incredible country.

- The Wildlife

    And I'm not just talking about the exceptional wildlife that brings people to Namibia in the first place – the lions, giraffes, elephants, and rhinoceroses. Donkeys became a mainstay throughout my time in Omungwelume. I would see them every day in the afternoon and even got into the habit of saying hello as they sauntered down the dirt road alongside my house.

- Riding in the Back of a Pick-up Truck

    Whenever I got a hike into town, I loved getting rides in a pick-up truck and would immediately hop in the back. I enjoyed the hot air whooshing around my head and relished the smells of the desolate land. Even today, I'm convinced there is no better way to view the countryside than from the back of a pick-up truck.

- The Starry Skies at Night

    Namibia is one of the premiere countries in the world for viewing the stars of the southern skies. Sometimes late at night, especially during the dry season when there weren't many mosquitoes around, I would walk outside my house and stare up at the sky. Countless stars dotted the dark canvas above making it appear celestial. It's weird because I felt so far away from everything I had ever known, but at the same time, I had never felt closer to the universe.

- The Funny Names of the Shabeens
  Who knows how people choose the names of these tiny concrete bars. It was always a mystery to me. Yet they were creative names nonetheless. There was the Unlimited Adventure Bar, the Ministry of Drinking, Fanny Resting Bar, Plan B Bar, Gangster's Paradise, and even the Taliban Bar. Then there was my favorite shabeen name of all. It was located in the small town of Oshikongo, which bordered Angola. The name of the shabeen made no contextual sense at all, but perhaps that's part of the beauty of English syntax. Throughout the year, the other volunteers and I would joke about the names of different shabeens, but this one in particular always brought a smile to my face. The shabeen was called **Watermelon is Life**.

- My Moment of Zen
  Sitting outside in the late afternoon with a book and a glass of wine was my daily moment of inner-peace. I would watch the sun sink from the sky, and although I can't explain it, at the end of the day, everything in my life made sense.

- Showing Movies to the Learners
  The excitement the learners had when entering the dining hall for movie night was priceless. The intense joy they got from watching these movies will

forever be imbedded in my mind. The *Harry Potter* movies, especially, will never be the same.

- My Colleagues

  My colleagues at Eengedjo did a tremendous job of making me feel at home. Even though our group may have seemed inefficient at times, in the grand scheme of things, Eengedjo probably operated like a well-oiled machine compared to other schools. I was very fortunate to have been placed with such a fantastic group of people.

- The WorldTeach Volunteers

  The other WorldTeach volunteers were the glue that bound my emotional state together. During our occasional rendezvous, we shared our experiences and supported each other in times of need. No matter how far we grow apart, personally, professionally, or actual distance-wise, our experience in Namibia has forever linked us together.

- The Learners

  The learners were the most invaluable part of my entire experience, and I miss them to this day. I miss hearing the kids knock on my door at nine o'clock in the morning on the weekends. I miss watching them stare intently at my laptop screen-saver. I miss them stopping by my house to talk, ask questions, or just hang out. Heck, part of me misses seeing them try to sleep in class. I really miss all the learners I came into contact with at Eengedjo.

> Not only did they teach me the value of learning,
> they also taught me the value of teaching.

Fortunately, I left Eengedjo in capable hands. Another volunteer was due to arrive the month after I left. He was going to be the fourth consecutive WorldTeach volunteer at the school. I thought about the potential parallels between his arrival and mine. He would probably be given little time to acclimate, and soon enough learners would start showing up at his door inquiring about movies, pictures, and when he planned to open the computer room. I wanted the next volunteer to feel just as welcomed as I did, so when I found out his name I asked some of the learners to write welcome messages, which I taped to the wall in the living room.

The week before I left, I took down my own wall decorations. There were notes from the learners, as well as pictures I had put up throughout the year. As I started taking them down, it was the first time I was hit with the realization that I was actually leaving. They were memories I had been able to look at each day, reminders of the people I had met and the places I had been. And now, I was taking them with me.

So much had transpired throughout the year. I had participated in numerous cultural activities, such as drinking marula juice and slaughtering chickens. I had tried exotic food, like mopane worms, as well as African game like zebra, springbok, kudu, warthog, and ostrich. I had gone skydiving for the first time, jumping out of a plane over the sand dunes near the coastal city of Swakopmund. I had traveled around six different countries in Southern Africa. I saw everything from the tropical beaches of Mozambique to Nelson Mandela's cell on Robben Island in Cape Town, South Africa to the magnificent power of Victoria Falls at the Zambia/Zimbabwe border. Looking back, I wouldn't say that I found this part of the world, but rather, it found me. And for that I'm extremely grateful.

Living and working in Namibia has been an incredibly profound part of my life, and it has taught me invaluable lessons. It has taught me about patience, adversity, empathy, and excess. The experience has left an indelible mark on my character and has certainly changed me for the better. In the end, I feel as though I have a better understanding of my place in the world. And I knew exactly where I was meant to go next.

Chapter 23

Be the Change You Wish to See in the World

When it comes to volunteering, donating money, or giving aid, there are many conflicting viewpoints. The belief that people should be charitable and compassionate towards those less fortunate is ubiquitous. However, the manner in which it should be done is often disputed.

After my experience with WorldTeach, I wanted to help spread the word about some of the great work the organization is doing abroad. Therefore, I collected pictures and videos from all the volunteers and put together a video called *WorldTeach Namibia 2010 (Volunteer Teaching)*, which I uploaded to YouTube. I then posted a link to the video in a few different travel and volunteer forums along with a plug for the WorldTeach program. All I wanted was to share the experience. What I didn't expect was to get into a debate.

As it turned out, one person, whose screen name was Skyblue, didn't like that I was publicizing a charitable organization. This person's opinion is indicative of how some people feel about the word *charity* – skeptical. The primary complaint Skyblue had about WorldTeach was the costs associated to participate in the program. WorldTeach offers programs to numerous countries, and the costs vary because some programs are partially subsidized by the host country. In order to participate in the Namibia program, our group of volunteers had to pay $5,990, which included round-trip airfare, health and evacuation insurance, housing, training, and staff support. Regardless, Skyblue felt it unjust that organizations charge money for volunteer experiences while program executives earn nice salaries. In the case of WorldTeach, this is far from the truth. The problem was that Skyblue was casting aspersions on an organization which they knew nothing about.

There are many volunteer organizations across the globe that ask for assistance with their mission. Organizations may accept financial donations, and even offer programs where people can directly volunteer and participate in the mission. Opportunities may vary in duration and costs, and range from construction to healthcare to education. Since some organizations offer short-term programs and charge a hefty fee, I understand how people become cynical over such charitable business models. But any sort of volunteer work a person does will cost something, whether the cost is levied financially, physically, or psychologically. People just need to determine whether the rewards from the experience will outweigh the costs. Still, if you are going to discredit an organization, it's important to do your research first.

After we posted several messages back and forth, Skyblue stubbornly stuck to the position that WorldTeach was in the business of charity tourism as opposed to real charity work. Skyblue's claim was an individual's out-of-pocket expense for flights and accommodation, as well as having to search for a job, did not justify the WorldTeach program cost. I even explained that WorldTeach volunteers receive a $400/month stipend from the MOE, which over the course of a year just about covers the upfront expense. However, Skyblue continued to assume that WorldTeach is profiting immensely from these programs. In order to find out the truth, all it takes is a little research. According to *Charity Navigator*, a charity watchdog organization, WorldTeach receives high marks in their use of finances, accountability, and transparency. The organization spends 95% of its total budget on the programs and services it exists to deliver. Be that as it may, there are still naysayers and skeptics out there.

Debating whether or not certain charitable organizations are businesses would be arguing semantics. Many people who work for non-profit organizations earn an income, and sometimes donations are used to cover operating expenses so they can carry on with the mission. Of course, people are free to criticize those organizations they feel don't adequately support their mission. However, due diligence should always accompany one's scrutiny. Even though people like Skyblue choose to condemn the work of organizations they know very little about, others who may have been reading the forum might not easily distinguish between ignorance and sound judgment. As much I wanted to lambast Skyblue, I tried to keep the debate civil. If I were reduced to name calling, it would likely have detracted from the message I was putting out there. However, I'm now over my earlier reluctance.

Skyblue, you're an idiot!

"Eat your vegetables!"

This is a phrase young children may hear from time to time. Whenever adults want children to eat something, they try all sorts of ways to get kids to oblige. Some people may resort to guilt and pose the following question: "You know there are starving children in Africa?"

Of course, as a child I would have been more than happy to share my green vegetables with a starving African child. But in reality, there is no immediate connection between a child's vegetables in the developed world and hungry children in Africa. The food cannot magically teleport from a suburban home to a rural mud hut.[10]

---

[10] Mud huts are common throughout the northern regions of rural Namibia. They are small, circular houses constructed of branches and dried mud.

However, food can be provided by other means, though it's not. There are still many people in this world who are starving, even in countries as wealthy as the United States. And that is the real cause for concern – indifference. A statement regarding the *starving children of Africa* is a testament to our knowledge of the misfortune of others and our reluctance to act. Thus, the real question is not whether we should eat our vegetables. It is whether we should do something about helping those less fortunate.

In the early 1970s, moral philosopher Peter Singer of Australia wrote a well-known essay titled "Famine, Affluence, and Morality." The basic premise is that it is morally indefensible for some people to live in great luxury while others are starving to death. Singer asserts those who are capable of helping the poor should donate some of their income to aid those less fortunate. If we have the power to prevent something bad from happening, and can do so without sacrificing anything of comparable moral significance, we should do just that. He illustrates this thought with the following analogy: If you see a child drowning in a pond, you ought to wade out there and help the child. This would mean getting your clothes wet and muddy, which is an insignificant sacrifice. Thus, if we have the ability to make a significant increase in the standard of living of those at the very bottom at the expense of perhaps a small decrease in the standard of living of those at the top, then this would be a reasonable outcome. Singer's rationale is logical, and I think most would universally agree with the notion of helping others. So then why are there still many people living in deplorable conditions? As a global community, do we just talk about noble intentions but are reluctant to act?

The issue at hand is not whether we should help others, but how we should offer assistance. People want effective ways of making a positive change. But even nowadays, it is easy to cite forms of aid and assistance that have been utterly inefficient. People see money being poured into different countries and organizations that waste or squander it away. The world's problems then seem unsolvable, and people question the value of noble intentions. Perhaps this has contributed to our overall indifference and, as far as poverty is concerned, we have become "used to it" and have placed a symbolic distance between ourselves and those less fortunate.

When we examine poverty throughout Africa, the situation is a little more complex. Dambisa Moyo, a Zambian-born economist, has claimed that in the case of Africa, more aid is not the remedy. In Africa alone, approximately one trillion U.S. dollars of aid has been transferred to the continent from rich countries since the 1940s. Presently, the continent has little to show in economic growth and human development for such a vast amount of money. Moyo states as a whole, Africa is worse off today than it was 40 years ago in terms of the population living in dire poverty. On the other end of the argument is Jeffery Sachs, a well-known economist and large proponent of the United Nation's Millennium Goals, which were adopted in the year 2000 by all 193 United Nation member states. The UN Millennium Goals are eight development goals that strive to eliminate extreme poverty throughout the world by 2015. Sachs has called on developed countries to lead the way by stepping up their contributions of foreign aid. Therefore, it seems even prominent economists cannot agree on remedies of foreign aid. So if the "experts" cannot agree as to what should be done, where does that leave the rest of us?

Most Westerners have never visited the Dark Continent, so perhaps they feel that they cannot intelligibly get involved in a solution. But with modern technology at our fingertips, we can obtain the necessary information to make informed decisions. Charity evaluators such as *Charity Navigator* and *Give Well* help shed light on how people can support programs and organizations both domestically and internationally. Although no evaluation is perfect, it's a start. Today, our support is not limited to the local environment around us, but we can change lives from halfway across the globe with medicines, education, or even micro-finance. While at Eengedjo,

I learned that a church group in Colorado was supporting over a dozen learners with their school fees. It's likely these people have never been to Namibia, however, they were making a positive contribution in the lives of these kids. But what about me? What kind of difference was I making? Although I frequently questioned the futility of my work throughout the year, it wasn't until the very end that I felt I had an answer.

It's easy to romanticize the altruistic virtue of helping others. We tend to think just because a person volunteers they will become fulfilled with a sense of purpose. It's true if you do something good, you will likely feel good about yourself. But it's not always a win-win situation. The work can be painstaking, the living situation difficult, and the entire experience riddled with self-doubt. When living day-in and day-out as a volunteer, life is full of both rewards and setbacks. But in the end, the experience is really what the person makes of it.

Perhaps it is impossible to truly measure the value of my impact in Namibia. I partly feel that one year was long enough for me to realize I wasn't making a huge difference. There weren't drastic improvements in the learners' grades, and by the time I truly got settled into my new environment, the year was halfway over. It goes without saying a second year at Eengedjo would have been more fruitful. Thus, one could justifiably marginalize the influence of my presence. On the other hand, I could surmise that if I weren't there, then Eengedjo would have been short one teacher. My classes may not have been taught at all. There is no doubt in my mind there would not have been a computer class, and the room would probably have stayed closed the entire year. If that's the case, then I made a huge impact on the school. In all honesty, I truly believe I made a small contribution to the learners' education. And I'm humbled in making even a slight difference, as long as I feel it was a positive one.

An experience like the one I had in Namibia is esoteric, and for a true understanding one really needs to live it firsthand. Throughout this book, I've shared stories and anecdotes. However, I've really just scratched the surface. But my hope is that in scratching the surface, people might be intrigued to find out more. They will take that leap of faith in search of something new. They will seek out a unique experience in order to get a deeper understanding of the world around them and their place in it. And when we do this, what we discover is quite simple – change. I discovered the change in myself when I finally realized that perhaps one person cannot change the world, but the world can certainly change one person.

Posing with my 11D English class

Synchronicity

In early fall of 2004, I had just finished working a seasonal job in Alaska, where I had been saving up money to move abroad. Shortly afterwards, I traveled to Costa Rica on a whim to explore opportunities in Central America. Around the tail end of November, I began backpacking my way north into Nicaragua. Eventually, I found myself in a quaint little beach town called San Juan del Sur. I then discovered complete tranquility a few kilometers north of town at a beach called Playa Madera. The beach was serene simply because it was practically empty: just me, the sand, the sun, and a gentle breeze.

Normally, one would find a lot of surfers at Playa Madera, but on this day there were no waves to be had. The ocean was so calm I could have skipped stones across the water. Early in the afternoon, I grabbed a bite to eat at a small restaurant which overlooked the sandy beach. While waiting for my food, a little boy approached me at the table. He was a small, thin boy, with tattered clothes and no shoes. He came up to me and held open his hand, revealing numerous small seashells. Then he asked if I would like to buy one. I glanced from his hand to the sandy beach in front of me where there were thousands of small shells just like the ones in his hand. I told the boy I wasn't in the market for seashells, but if he wanted to sit down with me and chat, I would share some of my pizza with him. The boy tossed the shells back out onto the sand and took a seat at the table across from me. At this point, I was still learning Spanish and loved practicing with others. Therefore, I was more than happy to share some food in exchange for a bit of language practice.

The boy said his name was Johnny. He was 12 years old and from San Juan del Sur. After introductions, we discussed other topics pertinent to a Spanish-language beginner. I asked him about the weather, his hobbies, and what sports he liked to play. Johnny enjoyed talking about sports, and he was a big fan of soccer. He said his favorite player was Ronaldo of Brazil. When the pizza came, we continued talking about trivial subjects before moving on to more important issues, like girls. Johnny asked if I had a girlfriend, which I didn't, and then he told me he had a few different girlfriends in town. We chatted briefly about the women of San Juan del Sur and the boy spoke with the horniness of a shipwrecked sailor. Apparently, machismo in Latino boys begins at an early age. When I changed topics and asked him about school, he got a little quieter. He said he didn't go to school and wasn't really interested in it. I asked if he had brothers and sisters, but he confessed it was just him. When I inquired about his parents, he didn't respond and immediately changed the subject back to girls.

After lunch, I went to lie out on the beach and Johnny followed. Our conversation was starting to run dry. My language abilities prevented me from having an in-depth conversation, and all we seemed to have in common were sports and females. As luck would have it, while we were sitting there, two girls started walking our way. But suddenly, my wingman bailed. As the girls approached, Johnny stood up and walked off. He went over and sat down on a fallen tree at the edge of the beach. The girls weren't from Nicaragua; their milky white skin was a dead giveaway. One of the girls set her towel down nearby, and the other veered off towards Johnny. After a short conversation with the boy, she came back over to join her friend.

"He doesn't want to talk to me," she said.

"Just leave him alone then," the other girl replied.

Could these girls be his alleged girlfriends?

Curious about their relationship with the boy, I introduced myself and used Johnny as a conversation starter. One of the girls was from America and the other from France. We talked for a bit, and as it turned out, they were volunteers at an orphanage located on Isla de Ometepe, a small island in the middle of Lake Nicaragua. And that is how they knew Johnny.

Johnny had been living at the orphanage off and on for several years. He was there up until a few weeks before when he suddenly left. The girls didn't know particulars about his family background and speculated that he was probably sleeping on the streets. At any rate, the girls had the weekend off, so they traveled to San Juan del Sur for a little downtime. Apparently, they ran into Johnny the day before, and he told them he had been hanging around Playa Madera. The two girls were leaving the next day and offered to take him back to the orphanage. They also told me his name wasn't Johnny, it was Manuel. I suspected he probably wasn't telling the truth about his girlfriends, either.

During our conversation, Manuel watched us intently. When the girls got in the water, the boy came back over and sat next to me. He wanted to know what we had been talking about. I told him the girls said he was their boyfriend, but they were sad because he had left them. The boy just smiled while shaking his head. When I asked if his name was Manuel, he told me Johnny was his nickname. We talked casually for a little while, and eventually I asked if he would go back to the orphanage. Johnny shrugged his shoulders while staring out into the ocean. Soon after, the girls returned from the water and the boy retreated back to the fallen tree.

As the sun set, I decided to catch a ride back to town. I gathered my belongings, told the girls farewell, and walked over to say goodbye to Johnny. I wish I could say that I left him with some sage advice; however, I was so far removed from his situation I couldn't even begin to comprehend the hardships he had faced at just 12 years of age. I told Johnny it was nice meeting him and said that even though

I didn't know the two girls very well, they seemed sincere in their desire to help him. His response – "Women are crazy."

On that note, we shook hands, and I vacated the beach. I never saw Johnny or the two girls again. I always wonder what became of the boy. Did he return to the orphanage or take his chances on his own? For some reason, that day remains burned into my memory.

I never forgot the name of the orphanage, Nuestros Pequeños Hermanos (NPH). Ever since that serendipitous encounter in Nicaragua, I've followed the NPH website. The organization operates several homes throughout Latin America and has been in existence for over 50 years. NPH accepts volunteers for a variety of capacities, such as teaching, therapy, nursing, and caretaking. When I began my career teaching English overseas, I had always kept the organization in the back of my mind. I thought perhaps one day I might be in a position to offer my services.

After I returned from Namibia at the end of 2010, I had a few loose ends to tie up. I traveled to Asia for a brief stint, and then flew back to the U.S. in March of 2011. Ready for the next adventure, I filled out an application to teach English at one of the NPH homes. As fate would have it, the Dominican Republic responded to my request. The home was in need of an English teacher. NPH asked if I could arrive in the summer, so in June I left for the Dominican Republic. I was off to my new home – Nuestros Pequeños Hermanos.

Acknowledgements

I am indebted to so many people for the completion of this project. First, I would like to thank everyone who offered their suggestions, valuable insights, and humble opinions. I would also like to give a special thanks to Helen Gallagher, Denise Gates, and Brittany Dasher for combing through the unfinished manuscript for grammar and spelling mistakes, typos, and awkward sentences. Believe me, there were a lot.

Next, I would like to thank all the wonderful people I met while living and working in Namibia. You have no idea how much you enriched my experience. A heartfelt thanks to my fellow volunteer teachers who gave me an immeasurable amount of support. You truly made the experience unforgettable. In addition, my colleagues and co-workers at Eengedjo were incredible. They welcomed me at the school with open arms. I am also grateful to the hospitable people of Omungwelume. Everyone made me feel right at home. I was extremely fortunate and could not have asked for a better teaching placement.

Finally, and perhaps most importantly, I would like to thank all the learners at Eengedjo. I am so blessed to have met all of you, and I hope that I made even half as much of an impact on you, as you have made on me. I wish you nothing but the best and hope you continue on a pathway to success. You provided me with one of the greatest gifts of all – the chance to work hard at work worth doing.

Namibia is such an extraordinary and unique country. Even though I do not adhere to some of their cultural values, I am able to appreciate the diversity of tradition, norms, and way of life. I am sure I have left a mark on the country, but I have taken away so much more. Namibia will always have a place in my heart, and no matter where I go, I will always consider it to be one of several places that I call home.

The school grounds at twilight

About the Author

Wes Weston is a nomadic individual. Upon graduating from university, he backpacked across Western Europe, completed a thru-hike of the Appalachian Trail, worked seasonal jobs in Florida and Alaska, and spent a year in Costa Rica volunteering with Habitat for Humanity. Eventually, Wes discovered his passion.

With a love for traveling and being immersed in cross-cultural environments, Wes began a career teaching overseas. He has since taught in four different countries, including South Korea, Namibia, the Dominican Republic, and the United States. Currently, Wes lives in the San Francisco Bay Area, and is pursuing a Master's in TESOL. In the near future, he plans to resume his nomadic journey around the world.

Follow Wes on Twitter!

Like Wes' Facebook Page!

References

Winchester, Simon. "History of the Oxford English Dictionary." *TV Ontario* (Podcast). Big Ideas, December 2007.

"History of the OED." *Oxford English Dictionary.* Oxford English Dictionary, n.d. Web. September 2012.

Baron, Dennis. "The Gender-neutral Pronoun: After 100 Years still an Epic Fail." The Web of Language August, 2010. Web. September 2012.

"Top 10 Misused English Words." Listverse, June 2011. Web. September 2012.

Smith, Nico. "Namibia's Population Hits 2.1 Million." *The Namibian.* The Namibian, April 2012. Web. September 2012.

"Country Report: Spotlight on Namibia." *The Commonwealth.* The Commonwealth, May 2010. Web. September 2012.

"Namibia: Land Reform Reproducing Poverty." *Humanitarian News and Analysis.* IRIN, November 2007. Web. September 2012.

"WorldTeach Organization Information." *WorldTeach.* WorldTeach, n.d. Web. September 2012.

"Health Information for Travelers to Namibia." *Centers for Disease Control and Prevention.* Centers for Disease Control and Prevention, n.d. Web. September, 2012.

Van de Bosch, Servaas. "Heaviest Floods Ever in Namibia." *The Namibian.* The Namibian, October 2012. Web. October 2012.

"Evaluation of Promotion Policy Requirements in Namibian Schools." *National Institute for Educational Development.* Ministry of Education, March 2011.

Fischer, Gereon. "The Namibian Educational System." Friedrich Ebert Stiftung, September 2010.

Cambridge International Examinations. Cambridge International Examinations, n.d. Web. October 2012.

"Quality Primary Education." *USAID/Namibia.* USAID, August 2008. Web. October 2012.

Sasman, Catherine. "Quality, Shortages, and Concerns of Teachers." *The Namibian.* The Namibian, June 2011. Web. December 2012.

"Namibia: The EFA 2000 Assessment." *World Education Forum.* UNESCO, n.d. Web. October 2012.

Kisting, Denver. "Namibia's Language Policy is 'Poisoning' Its Children." *The Guardian.* The Guardian, January 2012. Web. December 2012.

Haidula, Tuyeimo. "Minister Iyambo Warns of Critical Teacher Shortage." *The Namibian.* The Namibian, November 2012. Web. December 2012.

Kleinhans, Godfrey. "Corporal Punishment in Schools." *The Namibian.* The Namibian, November 2012. Web. November 2012.

Smith, Anne. "The State of Research on the Effects of Physical Punishment." *Social Policy Journal of New Zealand.* Ministry of Social Development, March 2006.

Gershoff, Elizabeth. "Report on Physical Punishment in the United States." *Phoenix Children's Hospital.* Phoenix Children's Hospital, March 2009. Web. November 2012.

Borysenko, Natalia. "Chronetics as an Intercultural Principal of Translation." Dissertation. Web. October 2012.

Park, Andy. "Linguicide: How Dying Languages Kill Multiculturalism." *SBS.* World News Australia. Web. April 2013.

Allison, Peter. "Whatever You Do, Don't Run." *The Lyons Press.* The Lyons Press, 2008.

"Etosha National Park – Namibia." *The Cardboard Box Travel Shop.* The Cardboard Box Travel Shop, n.d. Web. November 2012.

"Victoria Falls." *SA Places.* South African Tourism Services Association, n.d. Web. December 2012.

"How to Turn 100 Trillion Dollars Into Five and Feel Good About It." *The Wall Street Journal.* The Wall Street Journal, May 2001. Web. December 2012.

Bond, Llyod. "Teaching to the Test." *Carnegie Perspectives.* Carnegie Publications, April 2004. Web. December 2012.

"Distribution of Family Income – Gini Index." *The World Factbook.* Central Intelligence Agency, n.d. Web. October 2012.

Brown, Rowland. "The Gini and Namibia's Three Wishes." *inamibia.co.na.* Umuntumedia, November 2011. Web. October 2012.

Heita, Desie. "Namibia: Unemployment is 28 Percent." *New Era.* allAfrica, November, 2011. Web. January 2013.

Measures of Effective Teaching (MET). MET Project, n.d. Web. December 2012.

Singer, Peter. "Famine, Affluence, and Morality." *Philosophy and Public Affairs.* Spring, 1972.

Millennium Development Goals: 2012 Progress Chart. United Nations, Department of Economic and Social Affairs. n.d. Web, March 2013.

6742931R00128

Printed in Great Britain
by Amazon.co.uk, Ltd.,
Marston Gate.